Biography

Nipsey Hussle

The life journey of a Hip-Hop legend

Brandie L McFarlin

The contents of this book may not be copied, reproduced or transmitted without the express written permission of the author or publisher. Under no circumstances will the publisher or author be responsible or liable for any damages, compensation or monetary loss arising from the information contained in this book, whether directly or indirectly. .

Disclaimer Notice:

Although the author and publisher have made every effort to ensure the accuracy and completeness of the content, they do not, however, make any representations or warranties as to the accuracy, completeness, or reliability of the content. , suitability or availability of the information, products, services or related graphics contained in the book for any purpose. Readers are solely responsible for their use of the information contained in this book

Every effort has been made to make this book possible. If any omission or error has occurred unintentionally, the author and publisher will be happy to acknowledge it in upcoming versions.

TABLE OF CONTENT

Chapter 1: True Story

Nipsey Hussle stood tall in the blazing Los Angeles sun, wearing an immaculate white T-shirt, a blue snapback cap worn backward, and a few kilograms of 14-karat gold Cuban links wrapped over his neck. Just behind him in the doorway of The Marathon Clothing smart store stood his big brother, Blacc Sam; his godbrother, Adam Andebrhan; his business partner, Fatts; and longstanding head of security, J.Roc. They were joined by hundreds of friends, family members, and special guests, including NBA star Russell Westbrook, Atlanta rapper 21 Savage, and Roc Nation's Emory "Vegas" Jones— not to mention Hussle's love, actress Lauren London. Slauson Avenue was closed for two blocks, west of Crenshaw Boulevard. The cops were outside. However, on June 17, 2017, the parking lot was filled with love.

"This was always one of our dreams, to be able to come inside," added Nipsey, who previously described the shopping centre at Slauson and Crenshaw to Forbes magazine as "a hub for local entrepreneurs." Neighborhood Nip honed his hustle on this stretch of tarmac, growing from a young G's perspective to an inspirational person in the community. Illicit transactions gave way to popping open his car's trunk and blasting his own self-produced CDs with Magic Marker lettering. "Just out of being' there for so long, we realised that it would make sense to be owners or have businesses,' ' he told me. "It was a major intersection with a lot of trade going on. And it made sense. If we can get in here, we'll be able to take what we're doing to the next level."

"Nip coulda taken his money and opened up a store anywhere," said L.A. radio personality Big Boy, who stood next to Hussle for the ribbon-cutting ceremony that marked the business's official debut. "But of course you know real recognize real and he chose to stay at the crib." Described as "the world's first smart store," The Marathon Clothing was unlike anything else in Hyde Park, a close-knit but economically disadvantaged neighbourhood in South L.A.'s west side. The new business was a quantum jump forward from their previous venture, Slauson Tees, which was a run-down beauty supply store with decaying carpet that Blacc Sam and Fatts purchased and restored in the mid-2000s. The technology, in addition to the hardwood floors, crown moulding, and a tailored retail experience suited for a Melrose boutique, truly distinguished the new venue.

Despite his humble exterior, Nipsey had every right to be proud. The Marathon Clothing grand opening resembled a circus on Crenshaw and Slauson. There were food trucks, inflatable bouncy castles for the kids, games, freebies, and homies riding their motorcycles and ATVs up and down the block. "If it wasn't for Nipsey, we wouldn't have nothin' around here for real," claimed one of the attendees that day. "All we need are Black people who work together to make things happen in our community..." "Nip for the hood and the family."

Big Boy handed the microphone to Marqueece Harris-Dawson, a lifetime Hyde Park resident who serves District 8 on the Los Angeles City Council. On behalf of the City of Los Angeles, he declared the event "the biggest grand opening of any business anywhere in Southern California today." In a private conversation with Sam and his family, the councilman mentioned that there are many CEOs who earn millions of dollars but would never attempt what this family firm has accomplished.

"Nip needs to be recognized by the city, man," his older brother stated. "Because he's doing something that most people can't do. And it is to rehabilitate an area, provide jobs for felons, and make motherfuckers productive. There are many corporations that cannot even achieve this.

The crowd roared as the council member handed over the microphone to "the one and only Nipsey Hussle." He waited for them to be quiet before speaking. "Y'all know how many years and damn near decades this has been in the making," Hussle continued, indicating with the enormous scissors he held. "We started in this parking lot as teenagers, when everything was abandoned..." There used to be a variety of things going on on this corner that no longer happen. Because some people over here changed the meaning of what this corner was about. "And you were a part of that."

As the throng moved forward and Nipsey proceeded on his train of thought, doing his best to explain all of his great concepts with his typical sense of urgency, the scissors became uncomfortably close to the heads of those in the front row. Big Boy reached up stealthily and removed Nip's massive shears. "I had a tight grip on those scissors," Nip explained as the audience chuckled. "Don't even worry."

Looking back on the grand opening ceremony is like remembering a magnificent moment filled with possibility and limitless potential. If only it were possible to turn back time and avoid the agony of March 31, 2019. "We launched that store together," Sandu explains. "He died in the same spot..." Directly in front. It was not in the store. He passed away on the same pavement where we cut the ribbon. It was extremely... He pauses, unable to find the right words. "These are all signs that the universe gives us."

"I can't talk about our last day together, and I still have to be strong for my children," London told GQ magazine eight months after his passing. "My three-year-old still asks, 'Where is Daddy?'" He does not grasp the concept of death. I haven't had time to process it all because it's too much, and I'm still working on healing myself and my family. But I simply enjoy the city."

"It's a blow for—not just the hip-hop community," Big Boy explains. "I believe that is a blow to all of us, just human beings. For our existence on earth. This is a terrible thing to happen to one of the best individuals, man.

"It's just sickening and disgusting," adds Councilmember Harris-Dawson. "Every time I think about it I get so angry that I don't have words."

Crenshaw, Nipsey Hussle's game-changing 2013 mixtape, concludes with a sorrowful three-part opus titled "Crenshaw & Slauson (True Story)." Although the project got greater attention for its unusual business model—selling a limited-edition CD for $100 while the album was available for free download—the music has held up well over time, particularly the final track. The tale, like all of Hussle's best work, is autobiographical, terribly honest yet also fiercely guarded. "The demonstrations speak loud so I ain't sayin' much," he tells himself. "No details till the statute of limitations is up."

Back in 2006, a fresh-faced twenty-one-year-old Nipsey Hussle, who had released his first "official" mixtape, Slauson Boy Vol. 1, the year before, attended the Hip-Hop Summit Action Network's "Get Your Money Right" summit on the USC campus. After taking part in a panel discussion, he paused to speak with famed Bay Area broadcaster Davey D.

Although Nip wore a thick gold chain and a little princess-cut diamond stud in each earlobe, his appearance struck Davey as subdued, at least for an up-and-coming rapper at the time. "How come you're not blingin' and having' all kinds of crazy diamonds and all that?" he asked the young man. "I guess you here to get your money right, huh?"

"All the time," young Hussle answered. "You know, all of it is great for the image, but all of it is a liability, do you understand? "I would rather invest in real estate."

"Wait, wait," Davey said, clearly shocked by the young man's intelligence. "Can you repeat that?"

"I said invest in some assets," Hussle repeated, this time louder. "As opposed to wasting my money on liabilities such as diamonds, you know what I mean? "Cars that lose value the moment you drive them off the lot."

"So you're trying to get land?" Davey approached Nip, who was still more than a decade away from owning the shopping plaza at West Slauson Avenue and South Crenshaw Boulevard, transforming the slogan "Buy Back the Block" into a viable plan of action.

"Exactly, homie," Hussle replied. "A real asset to take care of my people." Jewellery may seem nice, he reasoned, "but at the end of the day, it loses value. "It's not appreciation; it's deprecation." Although the teenage rapper was asked to speak at the financial literacy conference, he seemed more like a seasoned investment guru dishing out advice to everyone willing to listen.

Around 2006, Nipsey launched his own record label, All Money In, No Money Out. Much more than a catchy name for Hussle and his crew, All Money In was a mission statement—a self-empowerment formula founded on the notion of keeping every dollar earned circulating in the community, with the overarching goal of creating generational riches. Growing up in South Central, a once-thriving Black neighbourhood ravaged by decades of divestment and a policy known as redlining, which amounted to real estate apartheid, Hussle embraced these aims and propagated them as widely as possible.

Hustle and Gross opened Vector90, a 4,700-square-foot "coworking space, cultural hub, and incubator" housed in a former Wonder Bread factory five minutes from the Marathon Clothing store, one day before Victory Lap was released. The upper floor of the elegant space had a WeWork vibe to it, with reasonable pricing for paying members, while downstairs was a mixed-use area that served numerous community activities, including STEM workshops to help Crenshaw District residents prepare for science and technology careers. Lyrics from "Bigger Than Life," the hidden final track of Hussle's 2010 mixtape The Marathon, were painted in large white capital letters on the steps linking the two levels: "So, life is whatever you make it. I hope you start a movement. "I hope your opportunity survives the opportunist."

"In our culture, there's a narrative that says, 'Follow the athletes, follow the entertainers," Hustle told the Los Angeles Times on Vector90's first day. "And that's fine, but there should be something like, 'Follow Elon Musk, follow [Mark] Zuckerberg.'" I believe that being influential as an artist, young, and from the inner city qualifies me to be among those carrying that flag."

On the Victory Lap track "Dedication," Nipsey Hussle asks a serious question: "How long should I remain dedicated? "How long until opportunity meets preparation?" The remark was based on a quote ascribed to the Roman philosopher Seneca: "Luck is what happens when opportunity meets preparation." In his book Outliers, Malcolm Gladwell discussed the significance of preparation, developing the famous ten-thousand-hour rule, which calculates the commitment and diligence that Gladwell believes are required for success in any given sector. Hussle, an avid reader, read all of Gladwell's works. But he was well aware that no amount of planning would be of any use if opportunity never knocked.

Hussle, who grew up knee-deep in the lunacy that reigned in Rollin' 60s territory and throughout South Los Angeles in the years following the Rodney King judgement and the L.A. uprising, would occasionally ruminate on how things might have been different if he had been able to make alternative choices. Five years before he founded Vector90, he was asked what he would do if he wasn't in the music business. The twenty-eight-year-old offered a variety of possibilities, none of which involved illegal activity: "Something with technology, something with the arts..." I was always captivated by space. I'm not sure, but something entertaining and innovative."

Hustle told me a few weeks after Vector90's launch that having access to such a resource would have transformed his life. "My trajectory I'm sure would've been different," according to him. "I can't say exactly what, but I remember being fascinated and passionate about creativity and productivity from a young age. And out of frustration, I tumbled into the street. But if I had taken advantage of a handful of these possibilities sooner, the outcome would have been very different."

Hustle and Gross would cooperate on additional projects as well. Hussle, DJ Khaled, and Luol Deng participated in Gross's quest to buy the Viceroy hotel in Santa Monica in 2018, as did self-made Black billionaire Don Peebles, who sits on Vector90's board. Although the Viceroy agreement fell through, Gross was able to help Hussle and his brother literally "buy back the block" in January 2019, collaborating with them to acquire the shopping plaza at Slauson and Crenshaw where the Marathon Clothing business is located—and where Hussle initially started hustling. On March 31, their moment of success turned into sadness, but Hussle's death has only increased Gross' determination to continue their goal.

Gross rarely forgets how irreplaceable his business buddy was. "The range of his reach is what's unique about him," Mr. Gross states. "He could go to the Roc Nation Brunch with Jay and Puff, relate to them, and be respected as a peer. And then he could appear on Slauson and Crenshaw and be welcomed back here as someone who is still approachable and relatable. That is a pretty unusual thing. He inspired many individuals to become entrepreneurs, leaders, and business owners—and to do so with their own employees.

One of the lesser-known provisions buried away in Donald Trump's 2017 tax overhaul was the provision of significant tax breaks for investors in so-called opportunity zones. The benefits, marketed as a method to promote poor communities, were only available to those who pay capital gains tax and can afford to make fresh investments. The subsequent rush of funding was routed into locations designated by state governors in a secretive procedure that resulted in some questionable decisions. Trump dubbed Opportunity Zones the "hottest thing going"—but, predictably, members of his own inner circle, including son-in-law Jared Kushner's family, were first in line to reap the benefits, constructing luxury developments that would provide few jobs and accelerate the rate of gentrification, potentially displacing longtime residents. Inspired by Hussle's ethos of community engagement, David Gross established a campaign to use Opportunity Zones to inspire South Los Angeles people to "own our own." He dubbed the new program Our Opportunity, but the core idea was a twist on Hussle's incredibly simple strategy: keep all of the money in and none of it out.

Although Hussle did not win the Best Rap Album Grammy in 2019 for Victory Lap, his first nomination was a significant milestone in his journey. The next morning, he got up early to film the "Racks in the Middle" video. Members of the All Money In team, a tight circle of day-ones and handpicked talents from his hometown, were lurking about the video shoot's outskirts. Before dropping his first Bullets Ain't Got No Name mixtape, Hussle was developing the Slauson Boyz, a crew that included homies from Nipsey's section: Cuzzy Capone aka Yung Cuz, Cobby Supreme aka G-Bob, H60dsta Rob aka H&R, Rimpau the Rebel, Infant J Stone, Wee-Dogg, Tiny Boss Hogg, and Tiny Drawz.

It was the family's first visit to the Staples Center since Hussle's devastating memorial ceremony. Lauren appeared to the ceremony dressed entirely in black, from her outfit to her hair. Around her neck was a locket with a photo of Nipsey Hussle in his tux taken on the red carpet at the prior year's Grammy Awards. Lauren received the prize "on behalf of our family and in honour of Nip, who was a phenomenal vessel." His grandmother and sister joined her for another public event honouring Hussle. "Nip did it not just for the awards, but for the people," she said. "And God allowed him to use this music to speak his truth, give us wisdom, and something that we will forever be able to live with."

The man who stated "Fuck the Grammys until we get one" never had the opportunity to bring one home for his neighborhood, let alone apply all of the lessons he gained from the process of making his major label debut to all of the following projects he had planned. Nipsey Hussle thought he was just getting started, and that after focusing on growing his enterprises for so long, he had been making music with a "handicap." He was excited to increase the frequency of his music on his next two albums, which he was considering naming Exit Strategy and The Spook Who Sat at the Door, both with intriguing Trojan Horse undertones.

Hussle was not planning to leave when he did, but he was always prepared for any situation. Although he left no final will and testament, the proud father did establish seven-figure trust funds for his daughter, Emani, and son, Kross, to provide for them once his own earthly Marathon ended. In fact, when NFL great Reggie Bush launched a crowdfunding drive to help Hussle's children, the Asghedoms denied the gifts because the children were well-cared for. Hussle, a devoted father, never believed that money could replace his loving presence. Years later, on "Picture Me Rollin'," he reflected on the anguish of losing a parent, rapping: "It's never enough to console her / Telling 'Your daddy's a soldier' / She needs you right now in this moment / Not dead on your back pushin' roses."

Chapter 2: Slauson Boy

His mother, Angelique Smith, who worked long hours to raise her sons, did not prioritise "fresh" clothes over education. "She never told me no about a book," Hussle said later. "We might not go to Toys 'R' Us and get what I want every time, but if I am like, 'Take me to the bookstore,' she'll stop what she was doing and take me." Though young Ermias learnt a lot from his love of books, the streets of Crenshaw also taught him valuable things.

Crenshaw Boulevard, named for George Lafayette Crenshaw, a California banker and real estate mogul, spans twenty-three miles from the historic movie star homes of Hancock Park in central Los Angeles to the dramatic coastal views of Palos Verdes. As the city's burgeoning Black community congregated in the area that became known as South Central—their movements hampered by legal trickery, economic pressure, and threats of violence—Crenshaw became the main street of Black Los Angeles, lovingly known as "the Shaw."

Maverick's Flat, which became known as the "Apollo of the West" after the Lincoln Theatre on Central Avenue collapsed, would host prominent Black performers ranging from Marvin Gaye to Funkadelic, as well as personalities such as Muhammad Ali and Marlon Brando. Every Sunday evening, lowriders would roll up and down the Shaw, showcasing Los Angeles' thriving automotive culture. Ermias Asghedom was six years old when John Singleton's Oscar-nominated film Boyz N the Hood introduced Crenshaw to the big screen in 1991. As a child, he enjoyed seeing the Chevy Impalas, El Caminos, and Monte Carlos—and the occasional Cadillac Eldorado—ride slow and low, painstakingly customised to the last detail, blasting funk, soul, and hip-hop from their systems while bouncing on hydraulics. "Before we could drive," Hussle said several decades afterward, "a bunch of us kids would be chasing lowriders down the street, yelling out, 'Hit a switch! Hit a switch!'"

"My whole life took place on these four corners," Nipsey Hussle remarked, referring to his teenage years in the plaza at 3420 West Slauson Avenue. Before he could afford a car, Ermias would ride his bike up and down Slauson to see the action. "I mean, this really was my whole foundation," he claimed. "Everything." He even met Tanisha Foster, the mother of his first child, in the same parking lot.

Slauson Avenue, like Crenshaw Boulevard, was named after a wealthy white man—New York attorney Jonathan Sayre Slauson, who relocated west and established a bank, ran for mayor, constructed churches and orphanages, and planted extensive orange and lemon groves. The bustling thoroughfare named in his honour is more than twenty miles east of Culver City, the location of MGM Studios. Culver City was one of many places of Los Angeles designated as a "sundown town," which meant that any nonwhite visitors were advised to leave before dusk.

The systematic segregation of Black families is particularly reprehensible given California's rich Black history. The state was named after Calafia, a Black warrior queen immortalised in sixteenth-century Spanish fiction. California, which has been free of slavery since becoming America's thirty-first state in 1850, was formerly regarded as a beacon of hope for African Americans fleeing the South in quest of better opportunities. "Los Angeles is wonderful," declared author and activist W.E.B. DuBois. "Nowhere in the United States is the Negro so well and beautifully housed." The Mexican city of El Pueblo de Nuestra Señora la Reina de los Ángeles de Porciúncula ("Town of Our Lady the Queen of Angels") was founded by 44 people, mostly of African heritage, before California became a part of the United States. Vincent Guerrero, Mexico's first Black president, abolished slavery in 1829, decades before US President Abraham Lincoln. Pío Pico, a Black governor, took office three years later in Alta California. Pico, a self-made tycoon of mixed African origin, was California's wealthiest rancher for decades, owning half a million acres of land, constructing the most magnificent hotel in Los Angeles, Pico House, and inspiring the name Pico Boulevard.

Hussle recognized as a young man how city planners intentionally concentrated Black households south of Slauson. And, like in the Jim Crow South, segregation in California was maintained by violence. Beginning in the 1940s, racist groups such as the "Spook Hunters" terrorised Black persons who dared to visit white neighbourhoods. When the first Black family settled in Eagle Rock, northeast Los

Angeles, in 1948, a uniformed police officer joined a mob that set fire to a twelve-foot cross outside their home. Black families alleged racially motivated explosions and vandalism with no results. Black pupils faced the possibility of being ambushed while walking to or from school. The Spook Hunters donned coats with the image of a lynched person on the back. Young Black individuals started organising neighbourhood protection groups like the Slausons, Businessmen, Farmers, and Gladiators. Their sole objective was to defend themselves.

While they derived their name from a specific area, the Slausons were all about freedom of movement, opposing anyone who attempted to keep them from travelling the city. "We couldn't go here or there," adds Chinaman, another Slausons founder. "We are not gangs. "We are the pioneers who opened up Los Angeles." Other groups, such as the Businessmen, operated in a similar manner, resulting in conflict with police and groups from various neighbourhoods. Police from South Central's Seventy-Seventh Street Station were known for picking up members of one group and dropping them in opposing territory.

The death of Malcolm X on February 21, 1965, followed by the nationally published tear-gassing and beating of peaceful marchers in Selma, Alabama, who were attempting to exercise their right to vote, helped pave the way for the Watts Rebellion later that year. On August 11, 1965, California Highway Patrol Officer Lee Minimus stopped 21-year-old Marquette Frye near 116th Place and Avalon Boulevard. Frye was driving his mother's 1955 Buick with his brother. Frye had been drinking, and the officer arrested him, refusing to allow his brother to take the car home, which was only two blocks away. As a gathering gathered, Frye's brother walked home and brought his mother to the event.

It's difficult to say exactly what happened in those days before cell phone video, but a brawl prompted the crowd to throw rocks, resulting in six days of fire and mayhem. William H. Parker, L.A.'s notoriously racist chief of police, exacerbated the situation by referring to Black demonstrators as "monkeys in a zoo."

Chief Parker called in the National Guard, which had initiated joint training exercises with the FBI and LAPD the previous year.

Approximately 14,000 troops were deployed, including commandos airlifted in to occupy a forty-mile combat zone. When the smoke cleared, 34 people had died, more than 1,000 were injured, and 4,000 had been arrested, with an estimated $40 million in damage.

While President Lyndon B. Johnson later stated that "looting, murder, and arson have nothing to do with civil rights," many Watts residents saw the uprising as a success because it brought attention to issues hurting their city. "It was an absolutely transforming event," Mike Davis remarked, regarding "youth on the streets coming together and uniting with each other to drive the LAPD out." Rivalries between local factions were set aside. Grassroots activism and the Black Arts Movement, which included organisations such as the Watts Towers Arts Center, where young Ermias Asghedom would take music lessons years later, helped to heal the community by creating new creative opportunities and raising awareness of the issues at the root of the conflict. Following the Watts Rebellion, Black community organisations flourished around Los Angeles. Meanwhile, local street clubs and community groups increased their collaboration to protect residents from abusive police officers. Huey Newton and Bobby Seale launched the Black Panther Party for Self Defense in Oakland in 1966.

Rather than preventing violence, COINTELPRO's actions appeared to have the opposite impact. On April 4, 1968, Dr. King was killed in Memphis. On January 17, 1969, members of a rival group known as the US Organization opened fire during a meeting of UCLA's Black Student Union, killing Bunchy Carter and fellow Panther John Huggins. Carter's death at the age of 26 was a devastating blow to the Panthers. The question of whether COINTELPRO operatives were responsible for the shooting remains open, but there is no doubt that the FBI fueled the enmity between the two groups.

Something has to fill the hole created by the Panthers' "neutralisation." Around 1969, a high school student called Raymond Washington formed the Baby Cribs. Washington was born in Texas and raised in Los Angeles, near Seventy-Sixth and Wadsworth, just west of Central Avenue. Washington, who was short and muscular, was well-known for his hand-to-hand combat abilities and dislike of firearms. By the early 1970s, he had joined forces with a young crew led by Stanley "Tookie" Williams, bringing together the East and West sides of South Central to establish what would become known as The Crips. According to Tookie's memoir Blue Rage, Black Redemption, the Crips were primarily high-school-aged lads who banded together to protect themselves from external threats.

The group's quick development throughout L.A. created friction and strife in particular communities. Youths from Piru Street, Harvard Park, Arlington Heights, and Athens Park banded together to form the Original Blood Family, an alliance of independent bands similar to the LA Brims and Black P Stones. Some of the early members had previously been children fed by the Panthers' defunct breakfast program. The Bloods were formed in opposition to the Crips and have been at odds with them since their inception.

Despite having a different leadership structure than the Panthers, the Crips worked hard to build on the party's early successes, founding the Consolidated Crip Organization, or CCO. "We come from a neighbourhood of the leader of the Black Panther Party, which was a neighbourhood called the Slausons," stated pioneering Crips member Daniel Bey. "Our neighbourhood was the one Bunchy Carter came from..." We were taught that we had the ability to shape our own future. Danifu Bey contributed to the Crip Constitution, which established the Crips' goals and transformed their name into an abbreviation for Community Revolutionary Inter Party Service. Over time, this acronym/mission statement would take on various forms. Nipsey Hussle favoured the term "Community Reprogression in Process."

"She was really big on keeping a tight family," Hussle said of his grandmother, Margaret Boutte. "And big on love." Margaret's family emigrated from Louisiana, and she relocated to California during the Great Migration. She was raised Roman Catholic and had eleven miscarriages before giving birth to her second child, Angelique. After being bedridden for the majority of her pregnancy, she recognized the daughter as a blessing and named her Angel. "Imagine if I had given up on my tenth and ninth miscarriages," Hussle's grandma would tell him.

Dawit Asghedom fled Eritrea to America in the 1970s, just before turning 20, in search of refuge from the war raging in his East

African nation. Eritrea, located between Ethiopia and the Red Sea, was an Italian colony from the late 19th century to the conclusion of WWII. After Ethiopia captured the territory about 1960, Eritrean rebels launched a thirty-year campaign for independence. "If you think about the Eritrean battle," Hussle said years later during an appearance on Eritrean television, "there are so many parallels that you can take from it. If you stand for principle and what you believe in, and you're willing to live and die for what you believe is right, you can accomplish the impossible."

Hussle's Instagram features a black-and-white shot of Dawit marching through the streets of Los Angeles with a group of young Eritrean males. He's wearing bell bottoms and an Afro and holding a sign that says DOWN WITH APARTHEID AND IMPERIALISM. In one corner of the placard are the initials EFLNA, which stand for Eritreans for Liberation in North America. Hussle captioned the shot, "I see you, Pops." It is not difficult to imagine where Ermias acquired his revolutionary zeal.

Hussle was inspired to shed light on his parents' relationship with "Higher," his Grammy-winning collaboration with DJ Khaled and John Legend, which became the first single released after his passing. "Pops turned sixty, and he's proud of what we've done," Hussle said. "In one generation he came from Africa young / He said he met my moms at the Century Club."

During the early 1980s, South Central Los Angeles became ground zero for the introduction of crack cocaine into America, which, combined with President Reagan's War on Drugs, set the setting for a statewide wave of arrests and killings. Texas-born cocaine kingpin Freeway Ricky Ross (called "the real Rick Ross") is often blamed for spreading crack throughout Los Angeles, resulting in a thriving criminal economy that spread addiction, murder, and Crip- and Blood-affiliated entrepreneurs across the United States.

Years later, Nipsey Hussle rapped about how "Reagan sold coke, Obama sold hope," and this is exactly what he meant. So, was the crack epidemic really a CIA conspiracy? Declassified data indicates that the National Security Council and the CIA orchestrated a complex multinational operation to buy Iranian weaponry with proceeds from the sale of narcotics transported to the United States from Central America. According to Washington lawyer Jack Blum, the former chief counsel for the United States Senate Foreign Relations Committee, cocaine trafficking in the 1980s evolved into a "mass-production huge vertically integrated business." Among the gangs trafficking drugs into Los Angeles was one that collaborated with the Contras. Blum confirmed that there were hidden airstrips. "Aeroplanes were flying in and out to supply the Contras. "These guys know they can come and go without being asked any questions." These secret government schemes not only exacerbated the scourges of addiction, violence, and incarceration in communities of colour in the United States, but they also resulted in the formation of Central American street gangs such as MS13, which is today regarded as one of the world's most dangerous criminal organisations.

If it's true that a person's name moulds their future, Ermias Joseph Asghedom has been marked for success since his birth on August 15, 1985. Ermias, in Eritrea's Tigrinya language, means "God will rise." His father chose the name, later explaining that his kid "was sent by God to give some love to bring us together."

Ermias and his older brother were only three years apart and grew up sharing a bedroom. "When my mom came into the room and he was crying', I got whupped,' " Sam said during his brother's burial service. "That was my little brother, man. And I just did my best to set a good example and ensure his well-being." In his 2008 song "Reality," Hussle says, "It was just me and my brother." "Look, my brother is my nigga."

They were fortunate to have each other because the area around their home was going through some difficult times. "The mid-1980s represented the nadir of South Central's already tumultuous history," said California State University, Northridge professor Josh Sides in his book, L.A. City Limits, about Black Los Angeles. "Fueled primarily by the wave of plant closures, black unemployment and poverty rates rose throughout the decade."

The Asghedom brothers grew up on South Central's West Side, in the Hyde Park neighbourhood, within the jurisdiction of the Los Angeles Police Department's Seventy-Seventh Street Division, which one resident described as "the last bastion of white supremacy."

Among the detectives stationed there was Detective Mark Fuhrman, who would become well-known for his role in the O. J. Simpson murder case. Starting in 1985, the year Ermias Asghedom was born, Fuhrman began conducting a series of interviews with an aspiring screenwriter. His astonishingly open words, which he never intended to be associated with by name, provide a glimpse behind the "blue wall of silence" and into the Seventy-Seventh. "They knew damn well I did it," Fuhrman claimed of the event in which he "basically tortured" Black suspects before lying to Internal Affairs about it. But they couldn't do anything about it. The majority of the guys worked on Seventy-Seventh together. We were close. I mean, we could have killed people and gotten away with it. "We all knew what to say."

Although South Central has since been renamed South L.A., N.W.A's harsh assessment remains sadly true more than three decades later, during the Black Lives Matter period. Eazy-E, Dr. Dre, Ice Cube, MC Ren, The D.O.C., and DJ Yella used songs like "Fuck tha Police," which was banned from radio airways and public libraries and received criticism from police unions and the FBI, to express their own and a whole community's discontent. N.W.A., also known as "The World's Most Dangerous Group," had a distinct sound thanks to Andre "Dr. Dre" Young's creative prowess and a mindset that matched the name of their record label, Ruthless. N.W.A. was not the first to rhyme about street life, but they popularised what became known as "gangsta rap" internationally. Efforts to ban "Fuck tha Police" turned N.W.A. into First Amendment heroes, and the song became a protest anthem that is still played today.

On hot summer days, the greatest place to cool down was the neighbourhood swimming pool, which required a dollar for admittance. "That used to be a mission to get a dollar, to put it together," Hussle recalls. "We'd ask the lady to let us help her take her groceries in, to give us a quarter or whatever."

Sam realised at a young age that his brother had a talent for making money by applying his intelligence. While Sam and his friends were busy washing cars, watering lawns, and cleaning up neighbours' dog faeces, Nip discovered other methods to get money. "He always had a scheme," Sam said. "We'd work hard all day, and it appeared Nip would only put in ten minutes and come back with two or three hundred. "We could not believe it!"

Every day, their mother would get up early, be woken by a rooster in a neighbour's yard, and commute to Kaiser Permanente West Los Angeles Medical Center. Ermias attended the Open School, an alternative elementary program with a varied student body located near her workplace. He demonstrated an aptitude for creative writing. At the age of seven, Ermias penned a short fiction titled "The Snow Monster" about four brave buddies, one of whom had his elder brother's name.

David, a classmate who posted these student essays on social media, described Ermias as "just a nice sweet smart kid I used to know."

Unfortunately, schoolteachers did not always acknowledge his intelligence in the classroom. "In third grade, I had a Korean friend who was incredibly smart. I made another friend who was Jewish. "They used to copy my work," Ermias said in an interview years later. While his peers were evaluated to see if they might participate in a special program for gifted pupils, Ermias was not offered the opportunity to take the test. When Ermias inquired, his teacher explained that children had to be selected for the unique curriculum.

Ermias was six years old in February 1992, when the teen rap duo Kris Kross released "Jump," which topped the pop charts for eight weeks straight. Like the rest of America's kids, he was soon Totally Krossed Out, gaining major inspiration from the pint-sized Atlanta rap artists Chris Smith and Chris Kelly, better known as Daddy Mac and Mac Daddy.

"I thought I was gonna be like Kris Kross," Ermias later admitted on the Rap Radar show. He started creating his own raps with a specific goal in mind. "My goal was by the time I was twelve, thirteen I would be signed and crackin' as a little kid," according to him. "I got frustrated when I didn't get turned into Bow Wow."

For a talented student who had been overlooked at school, the rap game promised a more level playing field where a young Black guy could be recognized for his abilities. But, just as Ermias' dreams of stardom were taking shape, the world outside his family's house became more chaotic. On April 29, 1992, only one day after the

Community Self-Determination Institute brokered a shaky truce between competing gangs in Watts, two dramatic incidents shook the community to its foundation.

Ermias was six years old when the riots began; his sibling was ten. Dawit Asghedom was an enthusiastic CNN viewer, so his sons were always exposed to current events. "We talked about it," said Hussle's friend and musical partner, Baby Gooch, who is older than Hussle and shared some of his own street experiences. "He knew what was going on, since he was sharp. Everyone was looking at the police violence and all that."

According to Gooch, not all of the destruction was random, as media stories suggested. "After a while, the second or third day, you had idiots just settin' shit on fire that was drinkin'," according to him. "But at first, what people were burning were places with which they had a grievance. One of the first locations they torched was the store where Latasha Harlins, a fifteen-year-old Black girl, was shot and killed by a Korean store owner over a bottle of orange juice.

Whether you refer to them as the L.A. Riots, the L.A. Uprising, or las quemazónes—the great burning—the events that began on April 29, 1992, could not have come as a complete surprise to anyone paying attention. Many of the inequalities that sparked the 1965 Watts Rebellion have still to be addressed decades later, thus the aftermath was only a matter of time. Those who had no other idea might always follow A Tribe Called Quest's advice and "Check the Rhime." Chuck D of Public Enemy famously said, "Rap is Black America's TV station."

While songs like "Batterram" and "Fuck tha Police" predicted the frustration that set Los Angeles on fire, the simmering embers fueled the blunt of Dr. Dre's solo debut The Chronic, which shattered new sales records and crowned Death Row Records the world's biggest rap company. The Chronic, which was recorded while the city was still burning and released only eight months later, became an American pop culture milestone. Snoop later revealed in Allen Hughes' documentary The Defiant Ones that he "went out lootin' and stole all kinds of shit and brought it back to the studio" while recording the album.

As commercially successful as it was raw, The Chronic took all of the anger and fury of the Los Angeles uprising to the pop charts, cementing Dre's status as a multi platinum hitmaker, bringing in Snoop as a charismatic new superstar, and sparking Death Row's meteoric climb. Death Row, led by Marion ``Suge'' Knight, a former NFL defensive lineman turned bodyguard and music mogul, brought new meaning to the term "gangsta rap." Suge grew up in Compton with deep ties to the Mob Piru Blood group (Tupac would eventually align himself with the Mob as well), but Snoop and Daz of Tha Dogg Pound were associated with the Rollin' 20s Crips of Long Beach. Big U managed the other half of Tha Dogg Pound, Philadelphia-born MC Kurupt, who represented the Rollin' 60s.

Artists such as Nipsey Hussle and Kendrick Lamar represented a new breed of West Coast rappers who bridged the gap between Los Angeles and New York. "Now you can't spell New York without Los Angeles," Snoopy says. "We are all together now. There is so much brotherhood, from gang to rap culture. Bloods and Crips are prevalent in my city and throughout New York. They all link with one another. You have brothers from the same walk of life, with the same mindset." If Death Row initiated the process of reconciliation, musicians such as Nipsey Hussle and YG saw it through to completion. Despite the fact that there were several bumps in the road.

Ermias initially felt the joy of hearing his voice over a beat while hanging out with his homeboy Jermaine Jenkins, who lived close on Sixtieth Street. Jermaine's mother used to drive Ermias to elementary school, and the Jenkins family even had a computer at home. "Back then that was big shit to have a computer!" Nip remembered years after. Through ingenuity and sheer willpower, the boys found out how to connect a primitive microphone to the machine, and before long, Ermy was rapping over Snoop instrumentals, fitting his own rhymes into Doggy Dogg's flows from Tha Doggfather.

However, a bicycle may be replaced. Ermias, nine, had larger objectives than simply travelling around his neighbourhood. He felt frustrated despite being gifted, ambitious, and having a sympathetic heart. "Growing up as a kid, I was looking for somebody," he said later. "Not to offer me anything, but to show me that someone cared.

Someone who was driving change and had a goal beyond their own self-interest."

By the age of eleven, Ermias had found a new favourite rapper. Tupac Shakur, raised by Black Panther Party members, was a poet, actor, and charismatic leader with a rebellious spirit who never backed down from a challenge and was not afraid to escalate. Pac had teamed with Snoop and released the famous double album All Eyez on Me in February of the following year, after Suge Knight got him out of prison to sign with Death Row in October 1995. Then he heated up the summer of 1996 with "Hit 'em Up," which featured his crew the Outlaw Immortalz. The venomous diss track fueled Death Row's musical feud with East Coast rival Bad Boy Records to a fever pitch.

Ermias spent much of his time as a student at Edwin Markham Middle School, home of the Soaring Eagles, on public transportation. If his mother did not drop him off, he would take the Los Angeles Metro's Blue Line to and from Watts, where his favourite teacher was Merelean Wilson. Ms. Wilson was born in Compton and worked at NASA before deciding to pursue a career in education. Like all great teachers, she had a knack of bringing out the best in her students. "It is important that our youths realise that the difference between the impossible and the possible lies in their determination," she wrote in an essay for the Los Angeles NAACP Youth Council. "To succeed—do the best you can, where you are, with what you have."

"I'm going to be a rapper," Ermias would tell her while tapping out a beat with two pencils, but he was serious about his studies. Ms. Wilson recalls him as a straight-A student who ate lunch with her to ensure he understood his homework. Ermias, twelve, placed a poignant inscription in her 1997 yearbook, writing in unsteady cursive handwriting. "To: Ms. M. Wilson. I will always adore you, even through the difficult moments and long days. His handwriting in her 1999 yearbook was a little looser, and the sentiment was more positive. "To: Miss Wilson," Ermias, fourteen, wrote, "You were my favourite teacher and friend at Markham. Please never stop teaching; everyone in Markham needs a little piece of you in their lives. Love,

Ermias Asghedom." He added "Class of '99'" next to his signature. "Whop!! Whop!!" I draw the year in large bubble letters.

Watts was a long distance from home, but Ermias was meeting new acquaintances in the area, including Killa Twan. "We first met on the streets," says Twan, who grew up in the Nickerson Gardens projects. Despite his passion for school, he did not attend Markham since he was expelled from the district in sixth grade, supposedly for a gun incident. "The older dudes used to come from high school from projects we didn't get along with," Twan tells me. Many students at adjacent Locke High School were Crip members, while Twain's projects were home to the Bounty Hunter Bloods. "They'd come fuck us up at the school and I wasn't havin' that shit."

Meanwhile, Ermias pursued his own musical interest, hoping to become a teenage sensation. His mother couldn't afford studio time, but she found him a free music class. On Saturdays, Mom would drop him off at the Watts Towers Arts Center to study with a professionally trained composer. "He taught us how to use the MPC, which is the beat machine, a sixteen-track recorder," Nipsey told reporters. "That was my first exposure to production." Ermias was able to generate an infinite number of drum sounds and samples by tapping on the MPC's four rows of rubber pads. But each beat began with the sound of a metronome counting down the time. Tick-tick-tick.

When he was twelve, his stepfather's father purchased the family a home computer, which eventually broke down and had to be discarded. It was a devastating setback, but Ermias refused to give up, studying the computer publications his grandfather had given them beside the abandoned machine. One day, Johnny returned home from school with a backpack full of computer parts. Sam, who preferred to keep their room tidy, was dissatisfied with all of the creative clutter and requested that his brother clean it up.

Building his own computer was simply one stage in Ermias' musical journey, which he would later refer to as his Marathon. "He ended up getting software and being able to record music on that computer," Sam says. "I remember hearing something that he recorded at a young age and I couldn't believe it." The composition was incredibly complicated and accomplished. Sam had to pull him aside: "Brother, did you write this?"

The next day, Sam decided to try his hand at composing music—just in case the skill ran in the family. "If bro did it," he muttered to himself, "let me see." Within two weeks, he had abandoned the concept. "It skipped me," he said with a smile. From that day forward, Sam knew his younger brother was special.

"Whatever you can do," Sam told him, "we believe."

Chapter 3: Hussle in the House

After celebrating his nineteenth birthday in Eritrea, Hussle arrived at LAX with newfound resolve. Prior to the trip, he worked full-time and rapped on the side. Without a way to have his music heard, he was pleased to sell CDs hand to hand. He knew how to earn money, and he made a lot of it, but his activities were not in line with a bigger goal. "I wasn't making a million dollars in the streets," he told me. "I ain't gonna tell that lie." Over the years, he had amassed well over six figures. If he wasn't at Crenshaw and Slauson, he was on Brynhurst or Tenth Avenue. He knew what it was like to travel out of town, make money, and perform at performances. He and Ralo, Rimpau, and Fatts had many stories about their missions to Atlanta and Las Vegas, but he had to pick a choice. There was a moment when he absolutely had the game on lock, working his way up the supply chain to the point where his daily routine consisted of cruising about the hood in his white Lincoln, picking up bags for $500 here and $1,000 there. It was not an awful existence. Even at the age of nineteen, Hussle had seen far too many of his pals imprisoned for playing football. He understood he had to retreat for his own safety.

Hussle had moved enough crates and stacked enough paper during the previous few years of hard work. He thought he could focus on the music again—and go all out this time. No matter how hard he tried to deny it, it was clear by now that hip-hop was his actual passion. It trapped him like Don Corleone in The Godfather Part III—just when he thought he was free, rap drew him back in. He prided himself on never lying in his raps, but getting into shootouts between studio sessions felt a touch too real. It was time for him to stop balling and focus on his creativity.

"It was hard for my ego," he said. "I was used to being that young fly nigga, taking my pick of any chick I desired. At every party and club, the spotlight was on me." No more smoking Kush all day and partying at night. Success would not come without sacrifice.

Hussle was known throughout the city for his white Lincoln with Alpina rims—the type with the lock and key. "They were like name-brand rims," he said with a smirk on the Rap Radar program. "You couldn't get to the lugs without unlocking them. "That was some teen baller shit." Lincoln was so famous that girls wanted to ride in it, and his business associates wanted to purchase it. "I'm not selling this car," he assured himself. "I'm winnin' in this car."

Hussle realised it was time to set up shop for himself. Standing there in the parking lot, he realised he needed his own studio. He called his man D-Mac, who had been trying to buy the Lincoln, to see if he was still interested. D-Mac didn't give him a time to change his mind before pulling up in his lowrider with a bag full of cash. "He gave me the cash," Nipsey recounted. "I gave him the key." Nip also sold the majority of his jewellery—those Cuban links were comparable to equities and bonds, but Hussle required liquid assets at the time. He had finished flossing for the time being. He was about to reconnect with his higher mission and get back on the Marathon.

He needed to maintain his energy level for the following leg of the Marathon. Hussle wondered if he was as serious about music as he was. He contacted J Stone, a teenage MC who had been recording mixtapes on a karaoke machine since elementary school. Hussle met him on some street trash, but when they took the time to cut it up, he could tell Stone was not playing.

Stone told Hussle about his older brother, who was killed when he was thirteen. Stone prepared a tape in his honour called The Streets Ain't Safe and distributed it at Crenshaw High. "That's when my music changed," Stone explained. "It started from the heart. That is where the pain in my songs stems from."

They discussed their future ambitions. "Man, this is what I'm on," Hustle explained. "I'm aiming to create my own label. I'd want to name it Slauson Boy Records." J. Stone's vision was similar. "Yo, that is tight. "I want to start my own shit, too," he replied. "I want to launch Low Down Records. I'd like to have artists, too."

Big U has been incarcerated since 1991 after attempting to rob an undercover sheriff's deputy posing as a narcotics dealer. He went home fourteen years later, determined to turn his life around. During his absence, he wrote the proposal for the initiative that became Developing Options. "Almost everything to a T that I'm doing to this day, I wrote it out—helping the kids, doing the music, the movies."

27

Having previously handled Kurupt, he recognized music as one of the primary areas he wanted to grow.

Big U took an immediate liking to Dexter, who gladly offered his skills and knowledge with him, just as he did with Cuzzy, Gooch, and Nipsey. Dexter photographed Big U and his family at their home and taught him and his staff how to utilise video editing software such as iMovie and Final Cut.

The first person to introduce Nipsey Hussle to Big U could have been his nephew, Tiny Drawz, who met him at Claustrophobic Studios in late 2003. "Bear Claw had put out a big compilation for the homies to show their talent," Drawz explained in a video interview with Kev Mac. "I just happened to be one of the young homies that was lucky enough to get on there along with Nip." Drawz was already familiar with Hussle from his pop-the-trunk distribution tactics. "He had a hustle plus he had a flow."

When Big U, also known in the ghetto as Big Draws, returned from prison, he asked Tiny Drawz a simple question: "Who home?" There was a lot of meaning crammed into just two small words. The question "Who's home?" underscores the reality of high incarceration rates, the understanding that at any given time, a significant section of one's community will be behind bars. Big U, who had recently come home, wanted to know who the hottest talent was that wasn't currently incarcerated and was ready to make moves.

Tiny Drawz let him know. "You need to mess with Nip," he stated. "Nip might be the next one for real—the flow, the hustle, the image, everything." Big U promised to check him out, and Tiny Drawz kept nagging him until he did. "Music-wise," he replies, "that changed the hood a lot."

Cuzzy claims he was the first to come up with the idea for a rap gang called Slauson Boyz, after the renowned Los Angeles street organisation. "The Slauson Boyz is basically for the day-one people that were there from the beginning," Rob of Hoodsta states. "It's a little seniority with us." The important players, he claims, were chosen based on work ethic. Nipsey was the primary character. J Stone and Cuzzy were also fundamental members, and Tiny Drawz later joined them. Hoodsta has a studio where he was always working and recording everyone. "It was a big thing, bro," Hoodsta says. "It was fun!"

After returning from Eritrea, Hussle went to a local tattoo shop and had SLAUSON BOY tattooed on his back in large lettering. Nipsey took Dexter by surprise when he lowered his shirt to show off his new tattoo. "I was speechless, 'cause I knew what it meant," he relates. "Hold on," he said after a pause. "Let me just go get my camera." There was no dodging the problem now. Nipsey had actually put a hood over his back. Dexter's concerns remain unabated years later. "It was something he wanted," Dexter explains. "My perspective was, 'It's a reality around you, and you could use it, but I don't think you should go so deep into it.'" Nipsey had his own ideas about it. He was particularly keen in shaping his persona. Nobody advised him to put Slauson Boy on his back. He did it. It was part of taking ownership of a brand he was willing to live and die for. I wasn't very thrilled with it. I believed it was going a little too far down that route, and that it should have stayed more musical. But I think there will always be differing opinions on it."

After spending three months in Eritrea with his sons, Dawit Asghedom wanted to maintain communication with them. He could see the lads were going through a difficult stage in their growth. Police raided Slauson Tees and shut it down. But, as always, Sam found a way to rebuild by catering to a thriving DVD market. Meanwhile, Nipsey Hussle was altering the game by pursuing his musical dreams while navigating the dangers of street life. After selling his white Lincoln, he purchased an ancient Cadillac to move around in. One day, shots were fired, and a bullet passed straight through the car without striking him.

The hood used to hold regular meetings, but with so many arrests and the prospect of gang injunctions, the leadership structure was deteriorating. Knowledge was not being passed along as it once was. The Crips were well into their fifth generation at this point. Gooch labelled it the "Tiny Loc Era." They were the gangbanging equivalent of millennials: young, confident, and self-motivated, making decisions based on their own judgement and instincts. "They don't have their parents telling them to go to school and do this or that," Gooch informed me. "They seem to think freely. [Nip] was a free thinker who took advantage of the situation. And it's not easy to do or be that way. "That's difficult!" That was Nipsey Hussle to the T. Nonetheless, you were occasionally asked to contribute to the set. Hussle was upset by some of the tasks assigned to him, but he couldn't show it.

Sam decided it was a good idea to put some distance between Nipsey and the hood. The brothers bought a house on Western Avenue to reside in with their father. The house was four or five kilometres from the community, located on the border of the Eight Trey Gangsters, one of the 1960s' most despised adversaries. But that was part of the point: to go where no one expected them to be. It was time to switch up the vibe. And Hussle finally had the opportunity to set up his studio equipment.

Nipsey drove his bullet-ventilated Cadillac to pick up Cuzzy and transport him to the ETG residence. "He wasn't on fire all the way," Cuzzy remarked. "He was just starting a little street buzz, but the city knew him." Hussle was meant to maintain a low profile, but he did not appear to care.

The neighbours began to notice the music and home cooking. "Niggas started rollin' by," Robin Hood claimed in a Kev Mac interview, "and they were stopping. There were a pair of niggas that stayed catty-corner to him and were approaching the porch." However, Sam and Nip were aware of the hazards and were prepared to defend themselves with security cameras outside and firearms inside.

Nip invited Dexter to the house to capture him and Sam in their element. "I photographed them with guns in their hands, money counters," according to him. "I'm the only guy they ever allowed to do it. That was the depth of our bond." Hussle is seen standing by the window, staring outside like the famed Malcolm X portrait, but he is not posing. "It almost seems like fiction," Dexter remarked. "Photos of Biggie, Tupac, and Jay-Z were all on the wall. That young boy I captured looking out the window like Malcolm became what he aspired to become."

The fact that they knew what they were doing was legal let them keep going. "You ain't hear helicopters at night and think they were about to kick your door in," Hussle insisted. "You ain't have to have that paranoia that goes with every other hustle that we were involved in." However, the attack did not come as a complete surprise. However, this was not a narcotics raid. The cops were searching for DVDs.

Hollywood, like the music industry, had struggled to keep up with what studios perceived as digital infringement. Change was unavoidable as a result of technological advancements, and the film industry was divided on how to respond. Some believed that bootlegging had promotional value, attracting new viewers online and on the streets, but the Motion Picture Association of America disagreed. Under pressure to crack down on DVD bootleggers, the LAPD established a dedicated anti piracy team. They even arrested their own. Captain Julie Nelson, a twenty-eight-year LAPD veteran, was caught distributing counterfeit DVDs to an undercover investigator in 2003. A search of her residence yielded almost 250 illegal disks. Possession and sale were felonies.

It didn't appear fair. Not after all their hard work over the years. Not after Nipsey Hussle took a break from hustling to focus on music. "I was really just in the house working," he claimed. "Nobody knows how pure you are except you. But I was quite pure at the time. I wasn't doing anything but music... I was perplexed. "Where does good karma pay off?" To lose everything and then face criminal accusations seemed like too much to take. Hussle's faith was shaken, but he didn't have time to grieve the loss. His brother had a case to fight. They needed funds for a lawyer. He had no option but to hit the block again.

Hussle was familiar with the drill. It never altered. Fifty homies outside on the same strip serve smokers. Hussle had risen to some prominence before leaving the game, but now he is hustling hand-to-hand, a more difficult and less lucrative job.

On his first day back, Nip's friend Tiny Bodee expressed what everyone else was thinking: "Maaaaan, your shit flop, bro!" His remarks had the sting of truth. "My shit did flop!" Hussle informed himself. "I'm back out here swallowing dope when the police hop out." It was enough to make him rethink everything.

Before Sam went to prison, he gave Hussle his gold necklace with a diamond-encrusted Malcolm X pendant, one valued piece that was not stolen during the raid. Sam designed the piece and had it custom-made by a local jeweller.

"Malcolm X is somebody we got a lot of respect for, a lot of admiration for," Hussle told the crowd. "I respect what he represented. I respect the 'by any means necessary' mindset. I like his transformation from being a street person to becoming someone who had discipline and stood up for a cause that was and is still real."

"You can have that," Sam said to Nip. To him, it was more than just jewellery.

"Just a little something," Hussle replied. "Five hundred grams of 14-karat gold, half a kilogram. It's all about the content, my nigga. That's not what it is. It's not on me. "It is in me."

Steve Lobel, a veteran artist manager, grew up in Queens and began his rap career with Run-DMC. "I was carrying bags, driving vans, whatever I had to do," says the man who lives by the slogan "We Working." He worked his way up the industry, specialising in traditional New York boom-bap, such as the Beatnuts and Frankie Cutlass. He introduced Fat Joe to his future bride and assisted multi platinum producer Scott Storch in regaining control of his life and career after struggling with cocaine addiction. At the indie label Relativity, he collaborated with stars signed to Eazy-E's Ruthless Records, including Bone Thugs-N-Harmony, Three 6 Mafia, and Tupac's Outlawz. "I've had a thirty-year career, known a lot of artists," acknowledges Lobel. "I can confidently say that Nipsey Hussle was the smartest artist I've ever worked with." He was a learning machine. He studied books and sought information where many others do not.

Steve doubled back to the hood to learn more about the Slauson Boyz. He asked around until he met Cowboy, who led them to a booze store. He reached behind the bulletproof glass with a wire coat hanger and removed the last Slauson Boyz DVD from the display cabinet. Lobel enjoyed their no-frills music video. "Yo, this guy looks like Snoop Dogg," he joked.

"Yeah, that's Nipsey Hussle," Cowboy explained.

"What? Lobel responded, "I love that name." "Like Nipsey Russell, a comedian. "I have to meet this guy." Cowboy phoned his little friend.

"He pulled up about an hour later in a Caddy," Lobel recalls. "He had that Cuban link chain, long white tee, Dickies shorts, and high socks."

"See, that's what I loved about Nip," Lobel adds, recalling their first meeting. "He never changed anything except the size of his clothes. He grew into tighter shirts, yet he never changed who he was. He hammered on the hood wherever he went. Everything about him was true, from gang banging, business, and rapping to his hustle and work ethic."

"Oh shit," Hussle exclaimed as he got out of the bullet-riddled Caddy. "Steve Lobel!" Hussle, an intelligent student of the game and keen reader of rap magazines, was well aware of Lobel's contributions.

"Yo bro, I think you're a superstar," Lobel said, and they began rocking from there. The industry veteran wasted no time utilising his connections to land Hussle his first salaried job—in Japan. "They paid me to rap for the first time," said Hussle, who received a $10,000 cheque and an additional 20,000 yen to appear on a Japanese television show. "I ain't have no hell of a name," he said. "I don't even know if they knew the song I was performing." All he knew was that he had received a check to go to Japan.

A month after their meeting, Angelo called Nipsey again. "Dre's gonna fall back," he added. "He's not gonna make a move on that." Hussle assured him it was all love. "I just didn't know if it was the music, or his history with my neighbourhood," he stated following the conversation. After all, Dre had dealt with a lot of controversy between Suge and Death Row. "I ain't know what the reason was, but I respected Angelo for being a bridge, for getting him to listen."

Dre was not the only one who listened. Jonny Shipes, the creator of Cinematic Music Group, has recently secured a position at Epic Records. Shipes had discovered Sean Kingston, a Jamaican youngster residing in Miami whose song "Beautiful Girls" went on to become a huge pop hit. But what Shipes truly wanted to do was put out some good rap music. Cinematic, which was only getting started at the time, would later become one of New York's best indie hip-hop labels.

"Charlie Walk at Epic had given me a label deal and he was like, 'Go find some stuff,'" Shipes recounts. "At the time, West Coast hip-hop was not thriving. I contacted DJ Felli Fel in Los Angeles and said, "Bro, what the fuck is going on?" "Where's the hot shit?"

"Felli said, 'Well, there's this kid named Nipsey Hussle, but he's deep in the streets. I'm not sure you'll want to screw with that. "He's a real one."

When Shipes searched for Nipsey Hussle on Google, a Myspace page popped up. "There were one or two songs on there," he recalls. "'Bullets Ain't Got No Names,' and maybe he had 'I Don't Give a Fucc' too."

Shipes experienced chills while listening. "I felt like I was on Sixtieth and Crenshaw with him," he shares. He fell in love with the tracks' rawness, hard delivery, and sing-along hooks. Hussle painted pictures with every word he said. "It was the rawest shit I had heard in years." He hit Felli back, and twenty-four hours later, he and his associate Harlem MC Smoke DZA were on a plane to Los Angeles to meet with Hussle and his staff.

Before the Epic agreement was confirmed, Hussle and his management planned to release a mixtape. They titled it Bullets Ain't Got No Name Vol. 1. Steve Lobel had an excellent relationship with DJ Felli Fel from Power 106, who was also a producer and recording artist. He agreed to host the videotape. "Nipsey had a certain IT factor," explained Felli. "He had a lot of stuff, but much of it wasn't radio-ready. For me, it was simply seeing that Nip was exceptional. "I just gravitated toward his stuff."

Hussle was still not completely hooked on the Epic transaction. He persisted in pushing his management to seek better conditions because his ultimate goal was to remain independent. But then a situation arose that pushed his hand. He and three homies were apprehended in another police raid, and this one was messy. They were recorded on a surveillance camera with guns while partying with a female in a thong who was underage. "They charged a nigga with some bogus charges, homie," Hussle stated in an early Kev Mac video. "A nigga never did nothin' with the girl!"65 he said.

One of Hussle's friends had been detained, and he expected to be picked up soon. He talked to Big U, who helped him conceal. They decided to take Epic's latest offer and simply purchase the bag. Years later, on an online hit called "Respect Ya Passion," Hussle would rap, "My first record deal probably saved my life, so shout-out to my nigga Draws and Jonny Shipes."

"When I did my Epic deal, you know, I was on the run," Hussle admitted later. "I had a lawsuit pending. My crime resulted in incarceration. I assumed I was going to spend a lot of time." To close the sale, he sat in the house for three months while the paperwork was processed. "I figured if I went to jail and it was a real case, that's gonna be the end of my opportunity." Hustle and Robin Hood came to New York in January 2008 to execute the contract after Shipes informed them that the paperwork was complete.

After the transaction, they boarded an aircraft to Jamaica. Sean Kingston was taping a special for MTV's My Super Sweet 16, and it felt like the ideal spot to celebrate—especially since Hussle could face jail time if he returned to Los Angeles.

Hussle was visited by the gang investigation team once during his two months in prison. He pictured them questioning him about happenings in the neighbourhood, attempting to implicate him or pressuring him to reveal information about his homies. When he was led into the gang unit's office, he was surprised to find his Myspace page displayed on the jail computer. "They had my YouTube playing'," he recalls, smiling. "They were singing the songs too—by heart." You know you're popular in the streets when the gang unit enjoys your music. Hussle wasn't sure whether to laugh in their faces or sign autographs.

The notion that he was about to become a father was both thrilling and concerning. "My life did a complete perspective change because now... you are accountable," he informed me. "You are answerable for the well-being of someone other than yourself. This is a person. Things can happen that you cannot prevent. That you cannot take back. You must take significant precautions to protect your child from some risks. So my priorities, viewpoint, and agenda shifted a little bit. I won't say my identity or what I do changed dramatically, but my priorities and perspective did. My decision-making process now includes another element and factor. And that is my daughter's well-being. So there was a clear paradigm shift in the way I think."

Hussle first heard his voice on the radio after being released from county jail. "I had a team around me that had a good relationship with Felli Fel at Power 106," he told me. "He played 'Bullets Ain't Got No Names' around two weeks after I was released from jail. You sound different on the radio, and you know that more than a million people are listening. I was like, "Man...""

Hussle returned to New York for label meetings and to work on new music. Ships scheduled him for a recording session at the Manhattan Film Center, which is located at Sixty-Third Street and Park Avenue on Manhattan's posh Upper East Side. Shiest Bubz from Purple City Productions, a Harlem rapper, worked in the next room over and kept Hussle laced with nice smoke while he was in town. Hussle was having difficulty concentrating since every time the studio door opened, he could hear the beat Bubz was working on via the side of his ear. It was a supercharged version of one of Hussle's boyhood faves, Kris Kross' "Jump". "This shit is ridiculous! "I hope this nigga doesn't finish this song," Hussle mused. "I hope he sleep on this beat." He waited two or three hours until Bubz was ready to go home before approaching him. "Bro, what you doin' with that beat?' ' he inquired.

"I ain't doin' shit with that," Bubz declared. "This sounds like some Los Angeles trash. I was going to rock it, but this seems right up your alley."

Nipsey Hussle tried to seem calm, but on the inside, he was ecstatic. Don Cannon co-produced the beat with a Detroit-born producer known as Detroit Red, a play on Malcolm X's previous street hustler identity. "We slid that beat to 50," Don Cannon later told Hussle. "He picked another one." Hussle smiled and replied, "50 slept, man! That was dope, man. "Thank you."

Despite rapping with a gruffness reminiscent of The Game, Nipsey Hussle was often compared to Snoop Dogg. They had a striking physical resemblance and a cool manner, and they soon became close friends. They also had a Crip affiliation, however Snoop represents Long Beach and Game represents Compton. While rap legends Ice-T and WC have deep ties to South Central Los Angeles, both were born outside of the state and neither stated their gang affiliation as loudly as Hussle.

"Nobody said no hoods before Nipsey," Big U claimed during a Kev Mac interview. "That was the problem they were giving me in the industry with Nipsey Hussle—he's saying 'The 60s.'" He's not mentioning a city. He's mentioning a gang. And get this: if Nip hadn't signed with me, he wouldn't be allowed to say Six-Owe this, Six-Owe that."

Hussle had a buddy at KDAY, one of Los Angeles' largest radio stations, who told him about the number of calls from mothers the station was receiving. "Do you know what this record is saying?" they'd inquire. "He is from the 1960s. Playing this record promotes what's going on in Los Angeles."

"In my opinion, it is like, 'Nah, I'm not promoting it. "I'm just speaking about it," Hussle stated. "The radio people had to heed to that pressure and cut it off a little bit." Whether you hated or loved it, "Hussle in the House" was as unabashed as Hussle himself. He was not trying to hide anything. The song's chorus clearly indicated that it was "just a small introduction to this Nipsey Hussle music."

Chapter 4: Marathon Mode

Nipsey Hussle felt terrible when he received a call from Steve Lobel one February morning in 2010. "Nip, pull up!" said his boss, who would occasionally invite him on unexpected adventures such as BMX riding at the Fantasy Factory, a funhouse owned by professional skateboarder Rob Dyrdek.

"I'm sick, man," Hustle explained. "I'm in bed."

"Nah," replied Maniac Lobel. "Get up now. "Pull up!"

"Must be serious," Hussle told himself as he made his way to the address Lobel had provided. "It was all bigwigs there," he explained afterward. "I saw babyface and motherfuckin' Celine Dion. Man, everyone was there. If they ever bombed, it was it."

Just as he was thinking, "What the fuck am I doing here?" He noticed a familiar face: Snoop.

"Cuz!" Hussle replied, walking over to the big homie, whose managers instantly said, "Nip ain't supposed to be there."

"Well shit," Snoop responded. "Me neither!" When they argued that Snoop was supposed to be there, he responded, "Well, fuck it—we're both supposed to be here!"

Hussle had just seen his friend QDIII, who had produced a tune for Nipsey's forthcoming independent project. QDIII introduced him to his father, the renowned Quincy Jones. The artist who produced "We Are the World" for Africa in 1985 was now making another for Haiti 25 years later. And for whatever reason, he wanted Hussle on the album and in the video.

"Go get in it!" Q instructed Hussle, pointing to the studio.

"I'm cool," Hussle replied. "I'm just coming to show respect."

Q insisted. "Nah, go 'head!"

Hussle resisted, claiming he didn't know the lyrics to the song, but Quincy can be quite convincing. Hussle soon found himself surrounded by hip-hop legends, recording vocals with LL Cool J, Busta Rhymes, Kanye West, and Snoop. Despite his best efforts to blend among the crowd, Hussle stood out in his grey sweatshirt and iced-out Malcolm X chain. He even got caught up in the moment, flashing the 1960s hand sign. When Saturday Night Live parodied the song that weekend, they made fun of "half-famous randos like Bizzy Bone and Nipsey Hussle."

Hussle was not even upset when SNL busted their joke. Since leaving Epic, he'd spent a lot of time thinking about his brand, and he was clear that it wasn't about becoming as famous as possible. "Nipsey Hussle can't be Nipsey Hussle if he doesn't celebrate his successes but also his strategy," according to Jorge Peniche. "I believe that's what people gravitate toward. Nipsey is a natural motivator."

Even when he was still signed to Epic, Hussle worked like an independent artist. "I'm in overdrive, my nigga," he said. "A lot of artists accept the deal and become comfortable. You feel like that's what they came for, but I didn't come for the deal. "I came to connect with the people." As he embarked on a new chapter in his career, everything from his songs to his interviews talked of empowerment and redemption, revealing his experience as a young independent artist determined to succeed no matter how long it took.

"Really, I just want to convey what I have to say and communicate with my people. And give 'em some games to keep them entertained while telling them my narrative. I got a lot off my chest. I've been through a lot. A lot of my homeboys don't have any voice. "This story has to be told."

That summer, Hustle and Fatts embarked on a mini-tour of Europe and the UK. In August 2010, they were in London for Notting Hill Carnival, Europe's largest street celebration, and performed at an Eritrean youth gathering. He was being followed by video cameras, as he often was.

Hussle continued to work hard after returning to the United States, recording new music and establishing his business in his spare time. He didn't mind working hard on something he enjoyed so much. "Success to me is just being able to do what you love to do and support yourself off it," Hussle told reporters. "Live your dream and do what you enjoy every day. So I consider myself successful. I do not sell dope. I do not go to work. I perform music because I enjoy it, and that is all I need to keep going." Hussle attributed his success to "an aggressive, full-throttle approach" known as The Marathon. "Every day I run a lap and it doesn't stop."

When Hussle wasn't in the studio with his rhyme partners, he was working with Peniche to refine the All Money In brand's style. "With him going independent, it was such a big deal," Peniche added. "I was super excited to be part of that because it's like we had free rein to do as we pleased and innovate as we pleased and take our time to really roll out these elaborate or very comprehensive ideas that some people might not necessarily understand."

Peniche knew Hussle was a dedicated father and worried if he'd be happy being pictured with Emani. "I asked what he and his daughter liked to do. He stated she enjoyed being with him, especially sitting on his lap and pretending to steer his automobile. Peniche's harsh black-and-white images of a father and daughter bicycling through South Central were later shown as part of the hip-hop photography exhibition Contact High. Emani held the wheel while wearing heart-shaped sunglasses and smiling broadly. "The image to me was a homecoming of sorts, and an homage to success and fatherhood."

L.A. hip-hop had a significant metamorphosis following the Death Row era. Apart from Game, who profited from Dr. Dre's endorsement through 50 Cent, "gangsta rap" was not popular. "The clubs didn't support anything that was going on," said Chuck Dizzle of Home Grown Radio. "They wouldn't allow these guys to play shows because of the post-Death Row crap. West Coast hip-hop, in particular, has a negative reputation due to the gangbangin' stuff. These guys couldn't do shows and didn't gain radio play. So it simply dried up. And it was a circle of people going, 'What the fuck are we gonna do?'"

In 2010, L.A. rap got swept up in the jerk movement, with dance-oriented acts such as Cali Swag District and the New Boyz rising to prominence. "This new generation starts to come out with dancing and skinny jeans," Dizzle told reporters. "It created opportunities for individuals to spend money and think, 'Okay, this is enjoyable. I can invest in this. They were attempting to distance themselves from the stigma associated with gangsta rap. Street-oriented artists such as Jay

Rock, Glasses Malone, and Nipsey Hussle encountered opposition from both the industry and law authorities.

In late 2010, Cinematic organised a Smoker's Club West tour that ran from Vancouver to Arizona, starring Hussle, Curren$y, Dom Kennedy, and Smoke DZA. Everything went well until the December 8 event at the El Rey Theatre in Los Angeles. The LAPD proceeded to question the promoter regarding Nipsey Hussle's appearance.

"I had no idea how the gang injunction thing worked," Curren$y says, "but when we came to L.A., we couldn't have Nip at our event.

Nip was the one who told me, 'Yeah, if I come, they're going to shut it down until you get the LAPD to come do whatever.' I believe they smacked him and the promoters and said, 'Y'all can't do anything'.'"

Two weeks later, on Tuesday, December 21, 2010, the first entirely independent release from All Money In, No Money Out became available for download on iHussle.com. The official title of the mixtape was The Marathon (Music), however most people just called it The Marathon. To gain access to the content, new users had to register on Hussle's website, enter their contact information, and receive a welcome email explaining the project's philosophy: "The Marathon is all about the work before the celebration, the test of endurance that separates the winners from the rest."

The actual mixtape was delivered as a zip file comprising eighteen MP3s and a digital booklet in PDF format featuring images by Peniche, a track list, credits, and a note by Hussle. Blacc Sam, Fatts, Adam, and Nipsey Hussle are recognized as co-executive producers. Ralo Stylez was listed as an executive music producer.

The Marathon digital booklet included Hussle's essay explaining why he wanted to go independent. "As is the case with most people in this game," he added, "I am motivated by both financial and creative goals. I just had to make a decision about which motive I would prioritise in my job. Despite the fact that his company's name is All Money In, Hussle has chosen to value creative integrity over financial success. He claimed you could always tell when artists were going for radio hits and club bangers. Kanye West produced the song "Encore" from The Black Album, in which Jay-Z says, "When you first enter into the game, they attempt to play you. Then you make a few hits, and look how they wave at you!"

Hussle requested that Peniche highlight the following paragraph from his essay: "I WILL NEVER SAY SOMETHING I DON'T AGREE WITH OR BELIEVE IN... even if the reward is massive!". He went on to emphasise the values underlying his decision, which was not without sacrifice: "I always told myself that if I make it here I would keep it true to my heart and soul," said the writer. "I will not break my word for anyone."

The video for "Keys 2 the City" saw Hussle flying off in a helicopter and stunting atop a building while looking down at the Los Angeles skyline and the Staples Center. The first official single from The Marathon conveyed a clear message: Neighborhood Nip had advanced to a higher level. The song's lyrics listed all of the labels that have previously fronted for him, specifically mentioning Dr. Dre.

After establishing his own movement and leaving his major label agreement, Hussle began on The Marathon, asserting his independence while laying out a long-term strategy for success. In creating All Money In, he examined the blueprints of pioneers such as James Prince, E-40, Master P, Jay-Z, Biggs, and Dame Dash while developing his own master plan. "Not one person can make or break what I'm doing, except me or God," Hussle boldly said. "Not the label, not Dr. Dre, not Snoop, Game—and much respect to all them niggas, but as a man that's not how I was raised."

Soon after The Marathon hit the streets, Blacc Sam returned home from the pen and resumed his grind. Hussle's older brother had taken some hits, but he survived. "The house got foreclosed on," Hussle recounted. "That shop that he had originally, he lost it." Although Sam "had money put up," some of his plans were called into question. "He thought he had a situation to get back on his feet," Hussle told the media. "His credit lines ran dry. He had a foreclosure on his credit as a result of the legal predicament."

In the Victory Lap song "Young Niggas," Hussle mentions Sam burying a quarter million dollars in cash in their mother's backyard. "It was in an airtight safe, wrapped in plastic, fireproof safe," Hussle shared with me. "When he dug it up and unlocked the safe, a large portion—a little less than half—was moulded. Imagine a book, a moulded book, in which you are unable to turn the pages. "It was devastating."

Hussle, his sister, and mother plugged in blow dryers and assisted Sam in salvaging as much cash as possible. "It was wet, mushy, and soggy," he describes. "I didn't want to say anything because it was really difficult to obtain that amount of money back then. "It was a painful moment." The odour of moulded currency remained throughout the house. Some of the money had to be discarded, while some was barely usable. Hussle took a portion of it to the Slauson Swap Meet, making the best of a terrible situation.

Following his release, Sam jumped right into getting Crenshaw shirts printed, as seen in the "Hussle in the House" video. He put up a table at the Crenshaw and Slauson bus stop and began selling socks, T-shirts, and Crenshaw shirts in tiny batches—as many as he could afford. "We didn't make that a business at all," Hustle explained. That element of the vision was entirely Sam's, and as always, his instincts were spot on.

On the afternoon of March 18, 2011, officers from the Los Angeles Police Department's Seventy-Seventh Division responded to reports of a disturbance at 3420 West Slauson Avenue. According to the official police report, a "gang fight" broke out in the lane between the Shell station and the commercial plaza.38 "When the officers arrived, they saw about 10 gang members fighting and heard gunfire," according to the summary. "They also noticed one of the fighters, 29-year-old Samiel Asghedom, was in possession of a gun." Nipsey Hussle and Big U, who had previously collaborated closely, were among those fighting. Hussle was a fierce and seasoned fighter, but his tiny build could not compete with Big U, a massively built martial arts specialist. According to local sources, Blacc Sam fired a shot into the air in an attempt to end the conflict. Officer Salvatore De Bella fired in Sam's direction. Hussle recalls emptying a whole clip. "Police are trained shooters and do not miss..." He did not hit my brother at all."

After the smoke cleared, five people were apprehended and held at the Seventy-Seventh Street station, including Big U, Hussle, and his brother. Hussle responded to claims on Twitter, stating that he was not dead. I'm not in jail and not on the run. TMC."

"We've been through so many different tumultuous situations in the parking lot," Hussle said afterwards. "I believe there was a bigger purpose behind what we were doing over here. It was not to get into difficulty with the cops. It was not supposed to constitute a threat to the community. It was not to carry on a tradition of self-destruction. "It was to build."

Having disagreements is one thing; having difficulties is another. Hussle was questioned during a panel discussion following the incident if it was difficult for him to maintain contacts in his local neighbourhood as he got more prominent. "Your best friends can turn against you and become jealous," a person in the crowd said. "And it turns into a group of people trying to hold you back and keep you at the level you are."

The breakup occurred three months after the release of The Marathon, while the Epic agreement was still being finalised, and it marked the end of Hussle's working partnership with Big U and Steve Lobel. Hussle and YG had recently been in the ghetto filming a video, which may have exacerbated the situation. "It was a situation where the parties involved wanted to take advantage," says one set member, who spoke on the condition of anonymity. "The way that thing was put up, you'd come off like a bully out of nowhere. So you had to find a reason. This was one of those things. "Oh, you have a Blood in the Hood shooting a video?" The bottom line, as one Rollin' 60s member saw it, was that Hussle, Sam, and their father were resolved to stick together and fight for their rights no matter what.

LeBron James was in a zone. Standing in the home team locker room at Miami's AmericanAirlines Arena on June 12, 2011, he nodded his head to the song playing through his black headphones, ignoring the crowd of cameras and media members watching his every move as he went through his pregame routine. The Miami Heat needed to win tonight's game 6 of the 2011 NBA Finals. After a three-game road series against the underdog Dallas Mavericks, the "Super Team" containing three franchise all-stars—James, Dwyane Wade, and Chris Bosh—returned home behind 3–2. They needed to win today to force a seventh game and take the NBA championship they felt was rightly theirs. The pressure to win was nothing new to James. He was accustomed to it. However, this season has been difficult for a variety of reasons.

Since his surprising 2010 revelation that the two-time league MVP would be leaving his native Cleveland Cavaliers to "take his talents to South Beach" and join the Miami Heat, LeBron James has been disliked. Jilted Cavaliers owner Dan Gilbert referred to him as a coward, a traitor, and a narcissist, but James did not fit the "bad guy" position. "During my first seven years in the NBA I was always the loved one," according to him. "Being on the other side, they call it the dark side, or the villain... It was absolutely tough for me. It was a predicament I had never faced before. It took a long time to get used to it. It did not feel pleasant." He felt like he was changing into someone else. "I started to buy into it," he said. "I began to play basketball at a level or in a mindset that I had never experienced before. "I mean angry."

Hustle and James did not know each other at the time, although Nipsey did see the video as it circulated on the internet. "He ain't talkin' to reporters or nothin'," Hussle boasted. "He's just locked in." It was the kind of endorsement that money couldn't buy: one of the world's most famous professional athletes signing an independent mixtape artist. While game 6 did not go as James had hoped—Dirk Nowitzki and the Dallas Mavericks won 105-95, securing the Mavs' first NBA championship and humiliating the Heat—LeBron's endorsement could not have come at a better time for Hussle.

Given the significance of The Marathon, it was not surprising that athletes connected with the message. "They go through the same struggle," Hustle explained. "They just tackle it with their athletic abilities, whereas we do it with our art and music. So I believe that whether it's the message of motivation—whether they apply it to sports or just the quest of becoming better, bossing up and being successful, maximising your potential and challenging yourself—I believe those things are in the music and message of The Marathon."

Hussle was spotted in July 2011 at the luxury Palms Casino Resort in Las Vegas, courtesy of resident DJ Clinton Sparks. Hussle stopped shooting hoops at 5 a.m. to discuss the new music he'd been working on in the studio. "My last project was called The Marathon," he informed me. "I'm now working on a series of recordings. I haven't decided on a title yet, but it might be called The Marathon Continues, and it will be released for free. The release date is expected within the next two months, but could be sooner depending on how we work it out. I am in the studio every day. There aren't many features on this new one. Everything is kind of like in-house."

Hussle also performed in late July at the Las Vegas club Déjà Vu Showgirls for an event called the Strip Hop Topless Party. 50 Cent and Floyd Mayweather Jr. were in the audience when Hussle took the stage. Everything appeared to be going well—until Cobby Supreme observed some folks in the crowd acting fishy.

Hussle had not released any new music since The Marathon in late December, marking a purposeful dry spell. "The new music has a different sound," Hussle stated. "I kinda wanted to shock people with it as opposed to drop leaks and warm 'em up to it." The response to The Marathon indicated that he was building a devoted, engaged fan base. "Now kids tell me I'm the reason they finished school," he raps on TMC's new song, "Road to Riches." "And if it wasn't for The Marathon they wouldn't have made it through it." Hussle felt an obligation to uphold that standard, no matter how long it took.

He was still recording new material for TMC just days before the release date of November 1. "We're almost done," he remarked. "We're getting there." We practically got what we needed. I'm the type of artist who prefers to record at the last minute. My team could be a little unhappy because we have tight deadlines and such. However, it appears that you produce some of your greatest work during crunch time."

TMC's radical new style was obvious on the mixtape's second track, "Who Detached Us?," which was composed over a sample of "Rocketship" by Guster, a Boston-based alternative rock band. Hussle's lyrics raised enormous concerns about how his generation had lost its way, in broad language to which everyone could connect, whether they grew up in the hood or in Hollywood. "We used to be connected, who disconnected us?" Hussle inquired. "We used to be respected, now they are laughin'." Hussle stated, "If it was up to me, I'd rap like that on every song," implying that he had been repressing this aspect of his intellect in order to meet the expectations of his audience. He wasn't going to do it again.

Hussle celebrated the release of TMC with a live performance at the House of Blues on Sunset Boulevard on November 4, accompanied by the band 1500 or Nothin'.66 Hussle had known Larrance Dopson of 1500 since Robin Hood introduced them, and the production collective had a significant impact on the sound of TMC.

"We have been knowing' Nip' for a while," said Rance, a drummer turned keyboardist who was reared "in church in the hood" and moved into production when he discovered it paid more. "That's our brother," he explains. We grew up together. We've always done music, but Nip used to make his own tracks. We always had mutual respect for one another. And we all took the stairs, so we were climbing at the same moment." 1500 or Nothin' was a little further along in their climb at the time than Hussle, who regarded the band as "legends in the makin'." They were in high demand, collaborating with musicians like as Will Smith, Jay-Z, Kanye West, and even Dr. Dre's legendary Detox project. "They damn near worked with everybody that's anybody in the hip-hop world," Hussle said. "Their entire squad is extremely talented. And they're young and hungry. So I'm fortunate to be from the same area as them. I don't have to pay them $30-40 thousand for the beats! We are in-house."

Chapter 5: FDT

YG was winding up a recording session for his sophomore album, Still Brazy, in Studio City early on Friday, June 12, 2015, when "a little incident" occurred. His version of what transpired can be heard in the second verse of the song "Twist My Fingaz," which he recorded shortly after.

Less than two weeks later, he told a Billboard writer that he was "hard to kill," saying that the bullet that struck him "went in, went out, and went back in again," resulting in three wounds. "I can't die," he informed his colleagues, who rushed him to the hospital, smashing their car in the process. After changing automobiles, they arrived at the ER. Fortunately, the slug missed his femoral artery, and physicians quickly patched him up. After a brief interview with police, who described him as "very uncooperative," YG was free to leave the hospital the same night.The next day, he was back at the studio on crutches, and Nip came by to make sure his comrade was well. "I got shit to do," YG told Billboard. "This shit doesn't stop for nobody."

Trump was greeted onstage by his daughter Ivanka and stood in front of a crowd of media, inquisitive bystanders, and actors who had responded to a casting call, earning $50 to wear MAKE AMERICA GREAT AGAIN T-shirts and hold up placards of support. Then he told the first falsehood of his campaign. "Wow, whoa!" That is a huge group of people—thousands!"

According to reporters who covered the ceremony, there were maybe 100 individuals in attendance to witness the billionaire trust fund. The heir and star of the NBC reality show The Apprentice launches his campaign to become the United States' forty-fifth president. Donald Trump launched his campaign on a foundation of racial language. "When Mexico sends its people, they're not sending their best," he declared that day, deviating from the scripted talking points supplied by his staff and seemingly speaking from the heart. "They are introducing drugs, committing crimes, and raping. And some, I believe, are good people."

The candidate's foolish, divisive remarks were widely reported in the media, prompting Univision to cancel a $13.5 million arrangement to broadcast the Spanish-language versions of Trump's Miss USA and Miss Universe pageants in protest. His disparaging remarks should have come as no surprise. Trump had a well-documented history of racism spanning more than half a century.

In 1973, the United States Department of Justice sued Trump Management Inc. for refusing to rent units to Black tenants. In 1989, Trump purchased newspaper advertisements advocating for the death penalty for the Central Park Five, a group of youths of color who were wrongfully accused of rape and spent years in prison before being cleared by DNA evidence. Even after their names were cleared, Trump refused to apologize for inciting what amounted to a media lynch mob. In 1991, one of Trump's senior employees produced a book that quoted him as saying, "Laziness is a trait in Blacks." During President Barack Obama's first term, Trump promoted the "birther" hypothesis, claiming that America's first Black president was born in Kenya and thus ineligible for office. When Obama finally presented his birth certificate to counter the rumours, he called Trump a "carnival barker." The real estate entrepreneur and reality show star was suddenly vying to succeed Obama as head of the free world.

Although he had never been regarded seriously, Trump had pursued political ambitions since 1988, seeking the Reform Party ticket in 1999. After two terms, President Obama may have concluded that there were enough outraged white Americans to prepare the country for President Trump.

The atmosphere on the streets of America was tense. In the summer of 2014, police officers asphyxiated Eric Garner on a Staten Island sidewalk. Not even a month later, the murder shooting of Michael Brown in Ferguson, Missouri, sparked two weeks of violence between community activists and paramilitary police. That summer, following George Zimmerman's murder of Trayvon Martin, a statewide Black Lives Matter campaign emerged. Black Lives Matter moved on to rally support for residents of Staten Island, Ferguson, and other places where state-sponsored violence threatened African Americans' safety.

Two months before Trump announced his candidacy, Freddie Gray died in the custody of the Baltimore Police Department, sparking several days of protests. Maryland Gov. Larry Hogan proclaimed a state of emergency and mobilised the National Guard. Neither of the officers charged with Gray's death was convicted.

One day after Trump announced his presidential candidacy, Dylann Roof, a twenty-one-year-old unemployed ninth-grade dropout and self-proclaimed white supremacist, entered the Emanuel African Methodist Episcopal Church in Charleston, South Carolina—also known as Mother Emanuel—during evening Bible study and murdered nine Black parishioners with a handgun. He was captured quietly the next day and confessed to the mass murder, stating that the people in the church were so lovely to him that he nearly saved their lives. Prior to the bloodshed, Roof had complained to a buddy about the Freddie Gray protests, claiming that "Blacks were taking over the world." He is currently imprisoned in Terre Haute, Indiana, and is scheduled to be executed. In January 2020, attorneys appealing his death sentence argued that Roof "believed his prison sentence was irrelevant because he would be freed after a coming race war."

A few weeks after Trump began taking America on a lengthy escalator ride down, Kendrick Lamar sang "Alright" live at the BET Awards. "All my life I've had to fight, nigga," the great MC yelled, spitting truth from atop a graffiti-tagged pretend police car, surrounded by explosions and flames, with a large American flag waving behind him. Even after all of the hardships, horrible flights, and generally messed-up situation, Kendrick's song found reason to be hopeful. "If God got us," he stated, "then we gon' be alright."

YG, who first signed a deal with Young Jeezy, shared Nipsey Hussle's self-made ethos." "I'm the only one who made it out the west without Dre," he said during "Twist My Fingaz." He went on to establish his own 4Hunnid brand and secured his own label agreement for the release of Still Brazy. "Nip, we talked about a lot of family stuff, business stuff, life goals, brand goals," according to YG. Hussle offered insights from his studies and gave him a copy of The 22 Immutable Laws of Branding. Having survived such a close call, YG recognized the need of creating something that would last after him. "You ain't gonna be here forever," he told me. "So while you're here you wanna create something outside of your music that's gonna be able to take care of your family." YG regarded Hussle as more than a friend. "He ended up being like a big brother to me."

A group of thirty Black Valdosta State students chose to attend the Trump rally that day, wearing entirely in black as a gesture of "silent protest." Former KKK grand wizard David Duke had endorsed Trump earlier that week, so the students were naturally eager to hear what he would say on their campus. But they didn't have the opportunity. Before Trump began speaking, security agents urged them to exit the theatre.

"We didn't plan to do anything," said Tahjila Davis, a 19-year-old Valdosta State student majoring in mass communication. "They stated, 'This is Trump's property; it is a private event.'" But I have paid my fees to be here." Brooke Gladney, another Black student who was forced to leave, explained, "The only reason we were given was that Mr. Trump did not want us there."

Cell phone footage of the devastated Black kids being led out of the Trump rally emerged on social media, as did allegations that another group of Black students had been evicted from a previous Trump rally in Virginia that same day. Hope Hicks, the campaign's spokesperson, refuted claims of racial intolerance. "There is no truth to this whatsoever," she asserted. "The campaign had no knowledge of this incident." Her statement was challenged by Valdosta police chief Brian Childress, who stated that the campaign staff had requested that the students be removed from the event. "I'm not campaigning for anyone," the police chief stated. "That is not what I do." But in this situation, I support [Trump's campaign]. Chief Childress also published an official statement regarding the kids' ejection: "To suggest that this incident was racially motivated is unfair and simply not factual."

Tahjila Davis saw things quite differently. "I think we got kicked out because we're a group of Black people," she remarked in a televised interview, wiping away tears. "I guess they're afraid we'll say or do something, but we just wanted to watch the rally." And being kicked out because we are a bunch of Black people is insane. It demonstrates how racist our own school is.

Another explanation for Trump's ability to stay under the radar for so long, despite his racist history, was that hip-hop moguls were obsessed with the wealthy playboy whose name had become synonymous with success. Trump spent several years hanging out with Puff Daddy and Russell Simmons at extravagant rap events. In 2005, he stopped on 50 Cent's G-Unit Radio show to talk with DJ Whoo Kid and Tony Yayo. Donald mentioned that Ivanka was a big 50 Cent fan, and Curtis Jackson himself shortly called in to discuss. "Let's do a song," Trump told 50 people. "Write up some good lyrics." Yayo and Whoo Kid joked that they could call the single "You're Fired." Trump was proud of his hip-hop influence. Mac Miller, Jeezy, Smif-N-Wessun, and Rae Sremmurd have all released songs with "Trump" in the title. "I'm in more of these rap songs," he boasted. "My daughter calls me up, she said, 'Dad, you're in another one!'"

To his credit, Mac was one of the first hip-hop artists to criticise Trump's political career. In December 2015, he felt the joke had gone too far and wrote, "Just please don't elect this motherfucker man." In March 2016, the late MC made an appearance on Comedy Central's Nightly Show to underline his argument. "I fuckin' hate you, Donald Trump," Miller declared. "You say you want to make America great again. We all know what that means—ban Muslims, Mexicans are rapists, and Black lives do not count. Make America great again. "I believe you want to make America white again."

When Obama ran for president in 2008, the unified strength of hip-hop helped propel him to victory. Endorsements from rappers ranging from Jay-Z and Jeezy to Common and Will.I.Am, as well as two cover stories in Vibe magazine, contributed to record attendance among a diverse group of young voters. Eight years later, America was confronted with the most blatantly racist politician in contemporary history, but the mass opposition was disorganised. Someone needed to come up, harness the incredible power of hip-hop, and speak clearly, calling Trump out on his nonsense.

Hussle has put those beliefs into action over the last decade, bringing together people from all neighbourhoods and cultures on his crew, including his Mexican-born business partner and road manager Jorge Peniche. "The way Trump was campaigning was really affecting my guy," said Hussle, who now understands the power of Trump's speech. "His situation was very precarious. And watching TV, we're like, 'That's not right.' This dude attended college. This guy is a good person. "I witnessed it up close and personal." Fortunately, Peniche was able to resolve his predicament, but as the son of an immigrant himself, Hussle was aware that many others remained in danger.

Furthermore, Hussle had a huge Mexican fan following who attended his concerts and supported his movement. "I felt like they needed somebody to ride for 'em," Nip recalled! "Because we relate to the struggle, poverty, not having anything, and being incarcerated—we relate. So that message is not something we feel either."

By the time Black folks were being pushed out of Trump rallies, YG felt compelled to act. Trump was taking things too far. He mentioned it to Nip one day: "Look, bro, if we doin' a project called Two of AmeriKKKaz Most Wanted, we gotta have a song called 'Fuck Donald Trump.'"

Nip believed the concept was "tight," like a 2016 version of N.W.A.'s "Fuck tha Police." YG remembered his exact comments as follows: "Cuz, on Six-Owe, I feel you!" "Let us do it!"

Everything moved swiftly after that. YG knew exactly what rhythm he wanted to use. When YG explained the concept to DJ Swish, the producer assumed it was something he was doing for fun. "I never thought this would be popular," Swish said, "but it fits well with the times."

"FDT" meant more than just two rappers criticising a contentious politician. A Blood and a Crip had collaborated on a song dedicated to Mexicans, whose street culture in Los Angeles predates the Slauson and Businessmen. Nip and YG went hard in their verses, but they still made room for open-minded white people to join the movement. If historian Mike Davis is correct when he says, "I don't think there's anything the police fear more than the end of gang warfare," then "FDT" must be their greatest nightmare.

An LAPD spokeswoman indicated that there was no violence on the set and that no arrests were made, but hundreds of people were told to leave.65 Meanwhile, YG and his crew were filming their scenes on the East Side, at Fifty-Sixth and Central. "Helicopters were coming at us, the SWAT team was on us." They called off the shoot while the cameras were rolling. "We like, 'What's goin' on?'" YG recalls. "It was crazy."

The entire event was broadcast on TMZ, drawing additional attention to the "FDT" wave. On April 13, Kobe Bryant played his final NBA game, scoring 60 points in the Staples Center to cap off a twenty-year career with the Lakers. Five days later, the "F.D.T." The video was uploaded to the Worldstar YouTube account. The visuals began with a statement from both artists, laid out in white writing on a black background, describing the meaning of the song.

"As young people with an interest in the future of America," Hussle and YG argued, "we must utilise our wits and CHOOSE who will lead us into it wisely. The year 2016 will mark a watershed moment in our nation's history. The question is, "Which direction will we go?" The statement concluded by encouraging viewers of the video to "register ASAP and choose wisely." The harsh black-and-white video, with occasional dashes of red and blue, quickly gained millions of views. It was not long before the authorities took notice.

"Secret Service hollered at the label," YG said to a TMZ reporter while waiting for a security check at LAX. "They asked if they could see the lyrics on my album... 'Cause I'm talking about it on my album, they gon' try to take it off the shelf." Following the publication of "Fuck tha Police" in 1989, the FBI wrote to N.W.A's label, Ruthless Records. The letter made no mention of any specific song by name, nor did it threaten any music with censorship. According to an FBI letter, 78 law enforcement officers were killed in the line of duty in 1988, and tapes like the one from N.W.A are both demoralising and humiliating to these brave police. But YG and Hussle have piqued the interest of another part of the federal government. The Secret Service is in charge of the president's security. They didn't even bother protesting to YG's label, Def Jam; instead, they pushed the situation to Universal Music Group, the company's parent.

Undeterred by the radio blackout, YG and Hussle doubled down by releasing a remix of "FDT" with G-Eazy and Macklemore, spreading the message to fans of the clean-cut white rappers. (The original version remained significantly more popular on YouTube.) While

Hussle and Boog stayed close to home to await the arrival of their son, YG embarked on a countrywide Fuck Donald Trump Tour in the summer of 2016, promising to contribute $1 from each ticket sold to victims of police violence. He didn't want to be accused of trying to use "FDT" as a marketing gimmick. "Nah," he replied. "I'm really out here for the people."

Karen Civil, Hussle's business associate, had previously worked for the Clinton campaign. "She had the celebration set up for Hillary," Nipsey claimed. Hussle, like many others, felt Hillary had it all under control. "When they said Trump won, I was in shock," he explained. "Almost how I felt when Obama won, but at the opposite end of the spectrum."

As the shock of Trump's victory subsided, YG focused on "knowing my rights, chasing my dreams, and taking care of people." The "FDT" experience had a significant impact on him. "I'm on that positive [stuff] now," he informed me. "We're playing for keeps and survival. We need to play chess; we can't be playing checkers. We have to motivate, but we also have to make our own actions and strive to stay afloat. "What else could we do?"

As the Trump administration settled in, lying about the size of the audience at his inauguration, detaining children at the US-Mexico border, and imposing a travel ban on predominantly Muslim nations, the term "FDT" gained fresh traction. "When he won, the song became that much more meaningful," Hussle stated. Global outcry over Trump's plans grew, prompting Hussle to write, "A wall would not remove hate, but rather expand it. And a ban will not protect us, but rather separate us. "These protests demonstrate that hate can never drown love."

Although "FDT" received little backing from mainstream radio programmers, creative hackers devised a plan to get the album broadcast by whatever means necessary. According to the Associated Press, in January 2017, regular programming on WFBS FM in Salem, South Carolina, was interrupted for fifteen minutes as "an anti-Donald Trump rap song that contained obscene language" played on repeat. Similar instances have been reported at radio stations in Seattle, Louisville, and San Angelo, Texas. The song's music video was hacked into a cable broadcast in Mooresville, North

Carolina. Hussle shared news reports of guerrilla support for "FDT" on social media, stating that a regional Mexican channel in Nashville and a Catholic programming station in Illinois were also attacked. Hackers exploited a security flaw in low-power FM transmitters. According to reports, several stations chose to shut down rather than face repercussions for running the anti-Trump song. The South Carolina station discovered the alleged hackers' IP addresses, which were reported to the Federal Communications Commission. WFBS responded to the event in a Facebook post, saying, "If [the hackers] do not like President Trump, then get a sign and stand on a street corner."

In some ways, "FDT" followed Hussle's path, relying on devoted grassroots followers rather than mainstream support. The song, like N.W.A's "Fuck tha Police," has become a protest anthem, and it continues to be so even during the George Floyd era. Hussle's pal O.T. Genasis used the song in an Instagram post titled Crip Walking in Front of the White House. But mainstream radio steadfastly refused to play it.

The next day, Hussle called Power 106 and chatted with J Cruz, host of The Cruz Show, where he had previously visited as a guest. "We gotta be radical sometimes," Hussle stated. "All of us." During the interview, he stated that he had never complained about a lack of support for his own records, but that he saw "FDT" as an issue larger than his own career. "It's something we stood out on a limb for." Hussle announced his Atlantic deal two months later, setting the stage for the release of his major label debut. But at this point, music industry politics were the furthest thing from his thoughts.

Other rappers did their own calculations. Eminem's dissing of Trump during a BET Hip Hop Awards "freestyle" generated a lot of buzz for his comeback album Revival, which was released two months later. However, he remained mute at a critical juncture in the race. Slim Shady has "Stans" across the country. Who knows how many people sat out the election—or secretly voted to make America "great" again? Hillary Clinton lost Marshall Mathers' home state of Michigan by only 0.3 percent in 2016, the smallest margin of any state in the 2016 election. Clinton certainly could have used those sixteen electoral votes.

Kanye's ongoing support for Trump—the picture opportunities, the meandering monologues, and the MAGA hat—would continue to perplex loyal hip-hop fans, including Hussle. "I really am a fan of Ye's music," he stated during an interview with Nessa Diab, one of Hot 97's most politically informed personalities. "I truly believe Ye is crucial to hip-hop. I just don't agree with that portion of his conversation."

The one redeeming feature of Yeezy's odd bromance with President Trump may be that it allowed his wife to get a presidential pardon for Alice Marie Johnson, a former FedEx employee who served twenty-one years of a life sentence for her role in a cocaine smuggling operation. Even still, West's backing for such a violent and divisive public figure is pretty much indefensible—especially coming from an artist who previously excoriated a US president on live television, stating "George Bush doesn't care about Black people" in the aftermath of Hurricane Katrina.

"Honestly, this is the truth," Hussle said to Nessa during the conversation. "You're trolling with that hat. We are aware of this. He's looking for some sort of reaction." Hussle, who was raised to value certain morals and beliefs, could not understand such a reckless pursuit of fame. "I ain't even part of that culture," he joked. "I grew up valuing love and respect over simply doing things because people pay attention to you. But that's the era we're now in."

Growing up with genuine loved ones in his life, Hustle knew he would expect a reality check if he ever ran out of money. "Me personally, I gotta go back to a real place," he was saying. "I am in Hollywood, I am in this funny-style-ass music industry… no matter how goofy and weird the shit gets, I can't make no move that my ground zero is gonna not respect. 'Cause I'm liable to them, still."Hussle was slated to play at Broccoli Fest in Washington, DC on April 28, 2018, in front of a crowd of 33,000. While he was at the nation's capital, it seemed fitting to end his set with "FDT." Even two years later, "whether it was Black, white, Asian, or anything in between," DJ V.I.P., Hussle's official tour DJ, stated of the song's popularity. "People of our generation haven't benefited from Trump's policies. So everyone turned up and had a nice time wherever we performed." Fifteen minutes before Hussle took the stage, his team discovered a photo of Kanye wearing the red MAGA hat trending on social media. "We changed up our visuals for that performance on a whim," V.I.P. recalls. "It was something that we were all joking about... and we ended up throwing it up on the screen." The audience at Broccoli Fest booed the image fiercely.

Whether it was Kanye backing Trump or radio stations refusing to support "FDT," Hussle had bigger goals than maximising his industry clout. "I think all of us as hip-hop artists, we gotta be liable," he said Nessa, whose partner Colin Kaepernick understands sacrificing career objectives for principle. "Even if you're not from the ghetto, no block, or no place with norms. You are a part of hip-hop. Hip-hop has a standard. And you must hold yourself to that standard or you will be rejected. And if you don't check yourself, you can lose your privileges."

Chapter 6: Victory Lap

Hussle's phone rang non stop following Crenshaw's victory. Around that time, he met with 300 Entertainment, a new record label headed by seasoned music executives Lyor Cohen and Todd Moscowitz.

Hussle was correct about one thing: "Rap Niggas" would be the first single from Victory Lap. He never questioned that. However, it would not be on top of next year—or the year after that. In truth, "Rap Niggas" wasn't released until December 1, 2017. What happened during those four years is a narrative of dedication, determination, tragedy, and the triumph of willpower and imagination over seemingly insurmountable obstacles. In other words, this is the life biography of Nipsey Hussle.

"Nip always wanted 'Rap Niggas' to be his first single," says Rance of 1500 or Nothin', who revised the song several times over a four-year span. "This is how I'm about to disrupt the whole music business," Hussle would remark. "Let everyone know what time it is. And then I'm going to catch their attention and reel them in to the important information that everyone should know."

"It ain't even a traditional single," Hussle said. "It is not for radio, but it must be expressed. It is in context. Everything's going on. It's everything I'm representing right now.3 More than having a hit track on the radio or being renowned, Hussle needed to simply state, "I ain't nothin' like you fuckin' rap niggas."

When Hussle declared, "I ain't nothin' like you fuckin' rap niggas," he demonstrated that he was truly "about that life" in a way that most rappers could not be. "Did niggas laugh at you in the beginning?" Snoop once asked Hussle about the specific hurdles encountered by artists who grew up in gang culture. Informing your homies on set that you're about to become a rapper can be a tricky business. "I didn't even tell people at first," Hussle admitted. "Until I got good music that I believed in, I wouldn't tell anyone that I rap. Rapping felt like being on the streets, like being an outcast. Calling oneself a rapper is almost like saying you're retiring. Like you're not with this anymore."

"Like you done with the hood," Snoop remarked with a knowing smirk. "You've found other things that are a little bit more relaxing, like golfing and rapping."

"Exactly!" Hussle responded. "You know, so I had to turn it up extra sometime, just to show, like, I'm not on no rap shit." Tupac once wondered, "Is Frank Sinatra a gangsta singer?" He probably knew a lot of mobsters, yet he never sang about Sam Giancana. Similarly, hip-hop is full of studio gangsters who "wouldn't bust a grape in a fruit fight," as Jay-Z famously stated in "99 Problems."

Even before Hussle's Marathon series, his early raps provided an informed critique of gangster life, discussing problems and solutions from firsthand experience to foster constructive conversation. "I have a lot of concepts and titles that revolve around the state of this violent world we live in," Hussle stated during the Bullets Ain't Got No Name era. "One second I have this standpoint, but then on the next record I might take a different standpoint and speak on this topic from the perspective of intelligence, of somebody that wants to change this problem, somebody that wants to resolve the conflict."

Rather than inciting controversy for the purpose of it or being embroiled in media disputes about music and morality, Hussle attempted to paint a more complete image for those involved in the gang lifestyle, as well as those who would unfairly judge them. "A lot of my homeboys, including myself, at a certain point felt like there were no options left," he recalls. "Like, it wasn't no other decisions to be made than the ones we made as far as gangbanging, as far as being in the streets, bringing violence to other niggas that got the same color skin as you, that come from similar struggles as you."

Hussle's most urgent message was that the current generation of gang culture in Los Angeles is an effect rather than a cause. "We didn't wake up and create our own mind state and our environment," Hussle said to the crowd. "We adapted our survival instincts." We don't want our mothers clothed in black standing over our coffins. And having to be a burden on our parents, calling collect and getting upset because motherfuckers aren't writing or visiting you, and so on. That is not the lifestyle anyone wants for themselves, but it is the result of the one we live." For Hussle, redemption was the true mission.

The marathon was never a spectator sport. As reflected by the name of his website, iHussle, Nipsey Hussle considered all of his loyal supporters as individuals running their own races. Victory Lap was always intended to be a win for both Hussle and his audience.

The approach appeals to Dr. Melina Abdullah of Black Lives Matter, who met Hussle and spoke with him about cooperative economics. She believes that some of that sense of shared fate has been lost in the decades since his death. "That's something that bothers me about the aftermath of his death," says the woman. "They're trying to lift him up as this super-capitalist, which is not at all in line with what I know his intent to have been." Not that there's anything wrong with owning good things—Rolexes, Cuban links, and fancy cars are fantastic. But Hussle's aim extended far beyond creating money for himself and his family. As Dr. Abdullah explains, "It was about empowering an entire community."

Hussle stated that he first discussed Victory Lap in 2012, therefore the title's meaning may have developed over time. "I just know I wanted my debut album, the one we went to retail with, to be called Victory Lap," Hussle told me shortly after the record's release. The victory lap, sometimes known as the "lap of honour," is a motorsports custom in which the winning driver makes one more round around the track, usually at a slower speed, to salute the fans and soak up their adoration. It was intended to be a communal experience.

Hussle initially envisaged Victory Lap as the final instalment of the Marathon mixtape series, which served as a motivator for many of his fans. "I wanted the album release to close off the Marathon trilogy," he informed me, "and to represent the end of the completely independent, doing-it-on-our-own mode, and going to a new partnership." The All Money In label's win would be "establishing a new partnership that was in our favour this time," Hussle stated. "And more in the direction of what we came in trying to establish."

Hussle first met with Craig Kallman, the chairman and CEO of Atlantic Records, circa 2012, long before Crenshaw was released. He respected the fact that Kallman was a former DJ who founded his own independent label, Big Beat Records, and allowed Biggie Smalls to become a label head in his own right, releasing artists such as Lil' Kim and Junior M.A.F.I.A. "We had been talking for a while once I got out of the Epic situation," Hussle told reporters. "I began doing Marathon mixtapes and touring. I had specific terms in mind upon entering the building. They didn't believe I could justify my terms at the time, which was likely correct. So I continued working."

Hussle began promoting Victory Lap as a mixtape after talking with several major companies. He believed he was close to a deal, which he intended to announce after Victory Lap and then transition into album mode. However, Hussle realised that record labels were unwilling to give him any control over his creative output. "They wanna give you a check," he said. "I told them keep the check, give me an asset and just market and distribute my shit." He preferred to be involved as a partner rather than receive a large advance. "Niggas couldn't do that," he explained. "It wasn't because the label didn't want to help me. Their companies' corporate structures do not allow for ownership. And I am insulted by that."

Hussle adjusted his plans on the fly. "I called an audible," he explained. "I knew in my heart that failing to stand up for what I believed in made me a worse guy. I felt it was racist. Like, I don't deserve this trash I just constructed for myself? Want to give me some money? Oh, because you don't believe I understand what the asset is? "You think I don't understand where the true value is?" His goal shifted, as did his concept of victory. "I didn't do a press release or tell anybody about it," he admitted. "I just let my demonstration speak." He explained that his Proud2Pay strategy with Crenshaw was just the beginning. "That's just a small piece of what my plan is."

Hussle chose not to make the news until he had fresh music to release. "Nobody knew that," Ralo stated. "But of course when you're with a label, it's gonna be in your best interest—not only in your best interest, but it probably is required—that you work with the producers that are already in bed with the company." As a result, Ralo was on the outside looking in when work began on Hussle's major label debut. "Me and Nip, we weren't talking," Ralo says. However, when he saw the Victory Lap track credits, he felt compelled to contact them. "I texted him and I told him 'Thank you,'" Ralo reported. "I was surprised by two songs that are on the project I co-produced."

1500 introduced Hussle to Mike & Keys, the production pair previously known as the Futuristiks. They first collaborated with Hussle on Crenshaw songs such as "Checc Me Out" and "Blessings." Since then, he referred to Mike and Keys as "the home team"; all they needed was their own playground. Following the Crenshaw tour, Hussle put a significant portion of the revenues on a new studio he dubbed "the compound." It wasn't cheap to build up his own studio, but Hussle has always prioritised ownership. "I believe in investing in yourself when you make money," he told me. "You could easily go to a lot of places, but I just feel like your foundation should be strong."

Hussle saw the studio as the culmination of a lifelong dream. He arranged his bookcases and filled his whiteboards with short- and long-term objectives. He couldn't wait to begin work. "Nip used to pick me up at seven o'clock in the morning every single day," says Money Mike of Mike & Keys. "Everything he accomplished, he was already three or four steps ahead of niggas in what he was trying to do. Even we are creating. He ensured that we were always together. Nobody ever talks about the fact that we are Black males. It's difficult to work together and be in the same location."

"It's super important to really tap in," stated 1500's Rance. "We exist in each artist with whom we collaborate. And it's basically simply a soundtrack for life.

In addition to Mike & Keys and the 1500 or Nothin' team, Hussle enlisted the help of renowned producers such as Bink! and L.A. icon DJ Battlecat to boost the creative chemistry surrounding Victory Lap. New songs were being recorded, while previously recorded songs were reinvented, enlarged, and given new life.

Hussle believed he was doing the best job of his life. "That's what I'm proudest of is the radical exercise that took place on this project," according to him.30 He was finally able to fully immerse himself and demonstrate his abilities. "You gotta mine for diamonds on the earth, and that's a dangerous job," stated the official. "People die." Hussle thought about the creative process in similar terms. "To mine for your art, you have to dig for them. Music is like that, but it's dangerous to go mining for your own value."

Hussle felt music to be a spiritual process. "Anybody that fuck with music long enough—if you don't cloud yourself and miss it—you gonna realize it's spiritual," he told me. "If you're tuned in and present enough, vibrations are the word. So the word has immense power. "It is real."

Victory Lap was primarily a collection of stories from Hussle's life. "You've put out so much music," Elliott Wilson asked Hussle on the Rap Radar show, "how come there is still so much that hasn't been expressed?"

Hussle's objective, even as he recalled his past difficulties and sufferings, was to inspire. He informed Mike and Keys, "I want a soundtrack for my penthouse." I want a soundtrack for my Maybach. I want a soundtrack for my office. I want to feel the same way I do when I wake up in my car, looking out the windshield. Not a nigga from the streets coming and succeeding, but a long-distance pursuit. Finally, embrace your victory. "That is how I want the music to sound."

The short-attention-span internet music media cycle is eager to use adjectives like "classic" and "timeless," which only have meaning over time. However, when working on his debut album, Hussle paid special attention to great music from the past in order to give it greater lasting power. Although he had no idea Victory Lap would be the only record released during his lifetime, he gave it his all.

Hussle and his team embarked on a European tour in early 2015.

"I felt at home," Hussle said during an explosive performance at the O2 Academy in Islington. "I felt as if I were in Los Angeles..." That is the most enjoyable aspect of this for me. You can gain media attention and money—clearly, money is the motivator. But when you receive true love from other people. Someone yelling your lyrics, that's real. That is one of the biggest rewards for your hard effort. It is reinforcement. "That is why we do it."

Hussle was looking forward to getting back to work in his studio when he returned to LAX. He couldn't wait to see how the Victory Lap sessions were progressing and to finish up the refurbishment. However, he would soon receive some bad news concerning the studio. Hussle had been paying rent to a man he believed was the building's owner. In reality, he was subletting the space. The All Money In team was still finishing up construction when they received an eviction notice giving them days to depart the property. "It was just some political paperwork shit that went bad," Hussle informed the audience.

He approached the owners and claimed that he had no idea the space was a sublet. He offered to pay a year's rent upfront. "They just said, 'Nah, we cool.'" "We're not really fuckin' with you," Hussle recalls. "They ain't really give me no reason." He attended court with documents, receipts, and bank statements. "I've never failed to pay my rent. "Everything was always on time," Hussle stated. "The judge like, 'Brother, none of that don't mean shit.'" On the third day, authorities arrived and expelled them from the compound.

"That set me back," Hustle explained. "We had to reassess the entire approach. We took a significant financial loss. In addition, we had become accustomed to the working environment. It everything fell apart in the middle of the procedure, so that one was particularly painful."

The way a person handles hardship says more about their character than how they celebrate victory. Hussle was given a variety of recommendations for how to exact retribution. "I'm gonna burn the building down," they said. "Let me fuck this building up." Hussle and his colleagues had completed the construction of the walls and floors. It would have been easy to lash out. "I just told everybody to chill," Hussle recounted. "We're not doing anything. "We'll just take that one for the team."

As much as it stung to lose the studio where he intended to finish Victory Lap, Hussle discovered another victory in how he handled the setback.

"They robbed me, in essence," Hussle claimed. "They took something from me." They ended up keeping a lot of the walls and structure intact for their next renter." Hussle might have easily retaliated. All he needed to do was say yes. Instead, he preferred to let the universe balance things out. "It's cool," he said. "I ain't even taking it as nothin' but a higher energy movin' me out of that space."

The Victory Lap sessions were moved back to 1500 Sound Academy in Inglewood. Hussle also rented a space at Paramount Recording Studios. He immersed himself in the creative process once more.

On August 14, 2015, the Northwest.Straight Outta Compton debuted in theatres around the country and remained at the top of the box office for weeks. F. Gary Gray directed the picture, which had a $28 million budget and was co-produced by Dr. Dre and Ice Cube. Throughout his career, people have told Hussle how much he resembled Snoop. He was the natural choice to play Snoop on the big screen. "Snoop called me," Hustle explained. "Before Snoop, Ted contacted me, one of his business colleagues. People had contacted Dre prior to Ted. Prior to it, F. Gary Gray, the filmmaker." Hussle told everyone the same thing: "They're idols and legends. And these are the people I grew up admiring and listening to. But I've studied branding. One of the principles is that you do not walk in the footsteps of a great guy."

One byproduct of the Straight Outta Compton chats was Hussle eventually getting into the studio with Dr. Dre, which had been a desire of his for years, whether he liked to admit it or not. "I just heard the soundtrack," he informed Big Boy. "It's going to be epic." And I would have liked to have been active in a capacity other than what I was. I did music for the soundtrack with Dre." However, Hussle's songs were not included on Dre's third solo album, Compton, which was released one week before the film.

Hussle did, however, appear as himself in the pilot episode of Rachel Bloom's critically praised CW musical comedy Crazy Ex-Girlfriend. Hussle's iconic cameo poked fun at rap-star machismo in the musical performance "The Sexy Getting Ready Song." Rachel's character, Rebecca Bunch, prepares for a date by squeezing into Spanx and tweezing and waxing her hair. Hussle appears in the bathroom rapping, "Hop on my dick in that tight little dress..." He comes to a halt abruptly when he discovers the mess on her bathroom sink. "God," he exclaims in disbelief. "This is how you get ready?"

Rebecca nods. "This is horrific. Like a terrifying film or anything. "Like some nasty, patriarchal bullshit." Hussle excuses himself. "Do you know what? "I have to apologise to some bitches."

"He was so sweet and so funny," said the show's co-creator, Aline Brosh McKenna. "He was just game," Bloom recalls of working with Hussle. "He brought his girlfriend on set, and I remember her thinking the song was so funny."

Hussle wanted Victory Lap to go above and beyond after putting so much effort into it. During the process, he became an obsessive perfectionist. "I listened to Quincy Jones' interviews," Hustle explained. "I was listening to how he mixed Thriller, and how they had eleven songs ready to mix. He listened back and said, "What are the weakest three?" They got rid of them. And since they got rid of those three, they got 'P.Y.T.' and two more monster records that you probably can't believe weren't on the album's original round."

Quincy was not available to consult on Victory Lap, but when Lauren invited Hussle to celebrate her friend Cassie's birthday on August 26, he drew the attention of another superproducer. "I've known Puff, but at Cassie's birthday party we had a good convo," Hussle remembers. "He was like, 'I'm in Los Angeles, man. Come through. Let us hear the music. So I carried the record over there.

Puff encouraged Hussle to delete some tracks from Victory Lap. "Nip, you've got a classic album," Hussle remembered him saying. "A lot of legends don't have classic records, brother. "I'm not just throwing that word around." Puffy told him, "I've been driving to there in the Maybach. I've been listening to it bar by bar. "Take a couple of these songs out, and it'll stand up." Hustle followed his advice. Puff also enlisted Scott Storch and Mario Winans to play on certain recordings, and he supervised a second session of mixing.

Hussle had to endure the loss of family time on multiple occasions in order to create such a significant body of work over the course of several years. "How much did you have to sacrifice to get to this point?" On-air personality Hardbody Kiotti asked Hussle when the Victory Lap promo run concluded at 97.9 FM. The Box in Houston.

"Man," Hussle responded, pausing to consider for a second. "Everything."

As an artist, entrepreneur with multiple businesses, and father, there were never enough hours in the day. "Everything gets tested," Hussle stated matter-of-factly. "Your relationships are tested. All of that. The kids are difficult to explain to."

Hussle revealed that he used to keep Emani away from the studio. "There were many men in the studio," he explained. "And it just was a certain energy I ain't want to necessarily overexpose my daughter to." But, given how much time he was spending on Victory Lap, he reconsidered his strategy. "This is my life," he said. So I can't separate my children. That can't be the reason we don't have time." He reflected on how many Bob Marley interviews he'd seen with youngsters in the background. "It's gonna be weed lit," he remarked. "It will be everything you try to keep your children away from. "But the kids will be right there on deck."

Hussle created a specific space for Emani to hang out in while visiting the studio, and he established some basic rules of conduct. "We ain't gonna talk like that with my daughter in here," he told me. Hussle arranged for someone to monitor Emani while he worked and provide her with cartoons and food. "She can kinda peep what I'm doing and get a better understanding," he told her. "'He ain't just avoiding me. "He's really here working."

Kiotti, a former artist and rapper who moved into radio, said one of his favourite songs on Victory Lap was "Dedication," for obvious and not-so-obvious reasons. "You gotta love this shit," he remarked. "It's a lot to come with this."

Hussle agreed completely. "One hundred percent," he said. "If you don't love it, you'll stop. You're going to hang up the towel, for sure. And if you aren't willing to die and lose everything, you will not make it. And you probably won't die. Do you understand what I am saying?

"You're gonna pass out before you die," Kiotti jokes.

"But you gon' have to be comfortable with dying' for this shit," Hussle remarked, not kidding. "It's like gangbanging. You can't be a true banger until you're willing to die and face life. You won't be able to function in this environment. Not to suggest that's what you want, but you're going to have to accept it as a part of life."

Hussle's music team would continuously ask about "Dedication" as mixtape after mixtape was released—Mailbox Money in 2014; Slauson Boy 2 in 2016, and No Pressure in 2017. "You sleepin' on that record, bro,' ' they would say. "I'm not sleeping on it," Hussle would say. "I'm just waiting' till I'm in the right energy to write the rest of the song."

Walking across the parking lot, Hussle came upon Kendrick Lamar, who had a stronger connection to Tupac than other California rappers. As a child, Lamar witnessed Shakur filming a music video in his neighbourhood. Since then, Pac has appeared to him in a vision, and his most recent album, To Pimp a Butterfly, had an extended chat with Tupac's ghost.

The premiere was filled with West Coast rap royalty. However, the film was only average. As much as the lead actor resembled Shakur physically, no actor living could match his compelling personality. Throughout the evening, Hussle had a lengthy talk with Snoop, Lamar, and his label boss, Top Dawg of TDE.

"Top of the Blood," Hustle explained. "He's from Bounty Hunters. He is from the Nickerson Gardens project. Snoop from Long Beach, he of Rollin' 20 Crip. Kendrick is from Compton. He grew up in the Piru area. I'm from the Rollin' 60s. So Top and Snoop, during their time, the politics were so intense that no matter how powerful they were, there were certain topics that were simply prohibited. You couldn't really get into these types of stuff. But now Kendrick and I are from a different period." Hustle and Lamar listened to Snoop and Top while talking about Death Row-era street politics, as shown in the video they'd just seen, which ends with Shakur's assassination at the hands of Southside Crips. "We saw what happened with Death Row," Hustle explained. "We seen what happens when gangbangin' spills into music and street politics finds its way into power positions. "You have the perfect storm for destruction."

After years of planning and preparation for Victory Lap, aiming for the right beat, the best mix, and the ultimate moment of inspiration, there came a time—as with every creative endeavour—when the sound of the ticking clock drowned out everything else.

Rance recalls the final Victory Lap workouts as a fog. "It was crunch time at the end of the album and we all went in and went crazy last week," according to him. He estimated that up to six tracks might not make the cut, including several that became album favourites. "We had a bunch of radio songs on there," he recalls. "And we tapped into the culture and things came out how they came out—for real for real."

"I had big records," Hustle explained. "I had a record with Cardi B, I had a record with Future." Songs featuring such bankable performers were almost guaranteed to receive considerable radio rotation and make an impression on the pop charts, but Hussle was more concerned with the purity of his concept for Victory Lap. "I wanted it to be just a person telling their life story over the course of an album," he recalled. That's why he always stated that he was signed to his own label, All Money In, and collaborated with a large label to use their resources, contacts, and expertise. Nobody was going to put pressure on him to abandon his artistic vision in search of a club hit.

One of the final Victory Lap songs to be completed was "Last Time That I Checked," Hussle's collaboration with YG. "I wanted to create something for the West Coast that they felt was specifically for them," Hussle said of the song, which he dubbed a "anthem for the streets and my generation."

But, according to Hussle's production team, the anthem nearly didn't happen. "I can honestly say, that was a song that never would've happened if France never woulda pressed," according to Money Mike. For nearly two years, the tune remained unfinished, with only a groovy 808 beat and a hook that resembled a lyric from Young Jeezy's Atlanta street classic "Trap or Die."

"I understand art reflecting life, but we grew up with art instructing life," Hussle stated about the song. Whereas some of YG and Hussle's previous records were on the ratchet side, "Last Time That I Checked" was written with the explicit intention of educating a younger generation about how two young Black men survived the streets of Los Angeles and found a way to turn things around and live a more constructive life. "After a while," said Hussle, "I felt like it was almost a responsibility for me to give the game up."

Having the circuit in place helped Victory Lap achieve a greater purpose, providing a sense of completion to the project. However, there was still something missing. Hussle wants to highlight major musical moments and Marathon milestones to adequately portray his tale. He recorded follow-ups to two landmark singles, "Keys 2 the City" and "Blue Laces," a Crip confessional that Hussle once intended to make into a movie.

He called Mr. Lee, the famed Houston producer of the original "Blue Laces." They had spent two weeks together in a New York condo provided by Jonny Shipes when they made the first record, and they had maintained a close friendship throughout the years.

Mr. Lee was pleased when Hussle called him in February 2017 and said, "Bro, make me a 'Blue Laces 2.'" Two days later, Mr. Lee returned the beat. He used the same sample as the original, "Hospital Prelude of Love Theme" from the Foxy Brown movie soundtrack. Mr. Lee enhanced Willie Hutch's vocals by speeding up the line "Aw baby it's been so long..." to create an ethereal sound, reminiscent of angels speaking in tongues. The captivating instrumental was as evocative as a bittersweet memory, creating a tense atmosphere that got Hussle's juices flowing.

Big Reese, a member of Mike & Keys' production team, was in the lab that night. Hussle characterised him as a San Diego OG who "turned into a real positive dude that came out of the struggle." They had grown close, and Reese had the kind of chemistry that allowed him to push Hussle creatively. "That's tight, Hussle," Reese commented after the first verse was recorded. "Where you goin'?" Nip informed him that he was leaving and would be back tomorrow.

"Don't leave," Reese advised. "Do the second verse right now."

Hussle returned to the booth and probed deeper, unleashing another stream-of-consciousness flow that spoke about Dr. Sebi, a herbalist and healer who died in a Honduran prison in August 2016. Lauren had introduced Nip to Dr. Sebi's dietary advice, and he discovered that they helped him feel considerably better. Hussle became interested in Dr. Sebi's narrative after reading about a court case in which he was accused of practising medicine without a licence and claiming to be able to heal AIDS patients using herbs and a dietary plan. Hussle, who found it strange that the topic had not received more attention, planned to make a documentary about Dr. Sebi's life and joked in interviews about threats to his own life since the pharmaceutical business did not want Sebi's natural cures to be broadcast. "You know how they play," Hussle stated during a radio interview. "Niggas is tweeting at me: 'Hussle, be careful! 'Your plane is going down. I'm like, 'Y'all niggas, ride for me.' "

"Blue Laces 2" was the first and only time he spoke about Sebi publicly, claiming that the herbalist's death in jail was punishment for "teaching health." (The doctor's family claims he died of malnutrition owing to horrible prison circumstances in Honduras.) The rest of the verse discussed Hussle's adoration for Rick Ross, his business accomplishments, and his involvement with the Los Angeles City Council.

Hussle felt his labour was complete as soon as that record was finished. "I knew that at the point I was at in my career, I wasn't gonna do nothin' else till I felt that I had an album with fourteen or sixteen great songs," he told reporters. "My entire strategy was that when it blew me away, I'd be prepared to move. When I listen to it from top to bottom and feel shivers and hear a person in the music, I'm ready to go. So when I heard it, I was like, 'Yeah, it's out of here.' "

Hussle was able to devote more time to his growing family after finishing work on the album. Kross "The Boss" arrived on August 31, 2016—a Leo like his father, with a birthday two weeks later. Hussle has always enjoyed being a father, even though it worried him at first. "Nobody ain't ready for that," he remarked. "Hell no." You do not know what to do. But you'll learn together. Mother number one has the instinct, therefore that will kick in. What's crazy about the kid is that he's not actually trippin'. A diaper, a bottle, and love—we're cool."

The decision-making process was the most difficult. "The fatherhood part is easy," he remarked. What was difficult was staying dedicated to the grind. "Dang, I gotta make hard decisions," he was saying. Birthdays and Christmas were unavoidable. "We'll miss the bag for that," he explained. "But I'm sure I missed a cheerleading' practice or a tournament, a parent-teacher conference—that's part of the game."

He would explain to Emani why he had to leave during a cherished family moment to pursue an opportunity. He spoke to her as an adult, and even when she expressed disappointment, he believed she could understand.

He became much more selective after having his own two children. "I'm a sniper," he explained. "I have two infants now—a girl and a son. If it's not about business or employment, I can devote that time to my children." He never questioned the sacrifices he made for his family.

Having Kross was an entirely new kind of excitement. "He was a little sumo wrestler," Hussle quipped about his son. "He stretched out, however. I suppose he'll be tall. Hussle grew to six feet three in his late teens. Seeing a tiny man about the house pushed his thoughts in new ways, including his perspectives on life in the hood.

When people approached Hussle for advice, he took it seriously. "I share my experiences with young people in my hometown. I talk to them like they're my son. I wouldn't tell my youngster to join a reputable gang just because it's exciting. I would give my son advice as if I wanted him to win. You cannot even regurgitate the current discourse. You cannot. "You must develop your own understanding of time." He would never urge somebody to put on the hood again. Even if he had made the decision himself, he couldn't envision Kross fighting in the back of the buildings while wearing a blue rag.

He believed that the instruction he would give his own son was valuable enough to share with the world. "It's about money, it's economic," the politician replied. "Without money, your opinions are powerless. So my advice to my young people is, "Start." Get connected with music. Pick up a camera and record a video. Even if your father wasn't a rap artist, creative disciplines remained entry-level meritocracies. "You can buy your laptop for a thousand dollars and attack it and start something," according to him. "I feel like just empowering the ideas economically is the quickest."

Hussle, Sam, and their father visited Eritrea for the second time in April 2018. This time around, his experience was quite different from his initial vacation home fourteen years ago. "They had a minivan waiting for me, so I drove into the country," Hussle recalled.

His passport and paperwork were handled in VIP style, and his family remained at a hotel. "It was dope just breathing the air," Hussle stated. Instead of three months, they spent just over a week, largely in Asmara, the capital city. Hussle was stressed for time. As soon as he arrived home, he'd start planning the Victory Lap tour. He had time to meet with Eritrean President Isaias Afwerki, and he also got to see his grandmother and cousins, whom he shared excellent meals with. He stood on the cliffs of Asmara, looking down on his father's hometown of Adi Kefelet, reflecting on all the changes he'd witnessed.

"Seeing the way the city and everything else has changed is gratifying," Hussle told TesfaNews, the national news agency. "I adore being here. The people, food, culture, and lifestyle are excellent."

Hussle compared hip-hop to jazz, stating that music in America was a representation of our experiences as black Americans. Even as an Eritrean-American, he felt a connection to this piece of African American history.

"My father is from Eritrea and we have always been in touch with our Eritrean ancestry and culture thanks to him," Hussle told the crowd. "However, we grew up in South Central LA our entire lives. So we were exposed to Los Angeles' gang culture. I was born in 1985 and grew up during the 1990s. The LA riots occurred in 1993. Rodney King, LAPD brutality, and all of the social concerns that arose at the time occurred in our neighbourhood."

"Are gangs scary?" Temesghen inquired. "Terrorising?"

"If you come from areas in which gang activities are common then that becomes part of who you are," Hussle told him. "I suppose the appropriate metaphor would be coming from a position of war. If you do, you are aware of conflict from a young age and, without realising it, become a part of it. Following that, these persons from war zones become active in a variety of activities. Some become fighters, while others become writers, singers, or politicians. Everyone, in some manner, forms a subliminal relationship to their childhood experiences. And gang culture is similar. The prevailing culture of South Central Los Angeles led to widespread participation in what began as self-defence. The terms scary' or 'terrorising' are reserved for those who are unfamiliar with it. But for those who develop in it, it is just a significant issue. It's been there for generations. It's risky. White gangs targeted black people. It developed as a type of defence for your own Black people."

Now that the Victory Lap was complete, Hussle began to reflect on the people who had assisted him along the way. One of the persons he contacted was Jonny Shipes. "From 2013 to 2016, we didn't really speak," Shipes recalls. "No bad blood; we just parted ways. He would comment on my Instagram, and I would respond to him. But we weren't the same as before. For five or six years, we were intertwined, talking every day, sleeping in each other's cribs, and doing whatever it took to get by."

Hussle then hit him at random one day in 2016. "Yo man, you did everything you said you were going to do," he told Shipe. "It's so impressive to watch what you've done, and I never got to say this to you, but I just wanted to thank you." Shipes has worked with many people in the music industry and did not anticipate spontaneous displays of gratitude. It felt nice. They caught up and made plans to meet. "Yo, next time you're in Cali, hit me," Hussle added. "I'll come out, scoop you." A few months later, Hussle met Shipes at LAX, picked him up in a Maybach, and drove him to the studio to hear Victory Lap. "I've got to make sure I don't get choked up right here," Shipes adds as the memories return. "The last two years were the same as the previous five. Just completely regular, "Yo, come by the crib, come by the studio..." It's Lauren's birthday, so stop by. We're going to have so much fun. I suppose that was just his method of ensuring that me and him were okay."

After years of making enlightened movements behind the scenes and pioneering novel methods to the entertainment industry, Nipsey Hussle decided to formalise this portion of his profession by launching the Marathon Agency in October 2016. The core of the team included Hussle's godbrother Adam Andebrhan and longtime Marathon partner Jorge Peniche, as well as two familiar faces from Hussle's inner circle—marketing and branding guru Karen Civil and rap industry A&R Steve Carless, who collaborated closely with Hussle on Victory Lap. Peniche recalls Steve Carless as "protective and territorial" when he initially started working with Team Hussle before the agency was formed. "We gotta make sure that no one comes in and poisons the ecosystem," he recalls thinking at the time.

"We collectively were a group that helped push Nipsey to the next heights," Civil explained to me. "Through the Marathon Agency, we were able to market, promote, and raise awareness for other artists. We also collaborated with Nicki Minaj, YG, Dave East, and Teyana Taylor—all of whom understood Nipsey Hussle's business approach and assisted them with various projects." The Marathon Agency also worked with Pusha T while he was supporting Hillary Clinton's presidential campaign.

"Nipsey pushed you to want more, to become more," according to Civil. "When I first started working on the Hillary campaign, I discussed it with Nipsey. You've always wanted to get his blessing—and not simply ask him. You've always wanted to hear his thoughts on it. Is it a good idea? Is this a bad idea? When you doubted yourself, he was the voice of reason and understanding. "He was our hope."

There were other signals of promise in Los Angeles that autumn. The American Civil Liberties Union filed a federal complaint against the Los Angeles Police Department the same week that the Marathon Agency announced its inception, alleging that the department's gang injunctions violated thousands of city citizens' right to due process. At the time of the litigation, forty-six individual injunctions were in effect, affecting almost 10,000 persons across a 75-square-mile area. People under injunctions can be detained for wearing specific apparel or for interacting in public, and the procedure of fighting the injunctions is lengthy and complicated. Violations of gang injunctions can result in contempt charges, punishable by up to six months in jail. Residents of neighbourhoods affected by gang injunctions were "basically subjected to parole-like restrictions without any hearing on whether or not they are actually a gang member," according to ACLU attorney Peter Bibring. "That violates any notion of due process."

Around the same time, just as Victory Lap was closing up, Hussle spoke with Vanessa Satten, the XXL editor who had placed him on the Freshmen cover. She had watched how he was bonding with YG and musicians from other competing sets and wanted to know if this mirrored bigger developments in Los Angeles street politics. "We've always had situations where people from different sides of the tracks would be able to find some mutual ground," Hussle told the crowd. "You had Snoop and Suge Knight collaborating and establishing Death Row Records. Even my huge friend Drew would support Suge."

"Was it different then?" Satten asked. "Is it easier now?"

"This gets tricky," Hussle told her, his comfortable manner shifting noticeably. "Let me tell you something about gangbanging. Gangbanging resembles a volcano. Never become comfy in a volcano. Do you understand what I am saying? It might go. It might blow up. So things never really calmed down. It's just peaceful. It's cool right now. However, it will go up again. Not to sound depressing, but it is the reality of the situation. So it may appear to have settled down, only to be followed by another sick-ass summer like this one. The summer of 2016 was particularly deadly in Los Angeles. Niggas died. Gangbangin' was crackin'. It's simply that sometimes it flares up and other times it's calm."

The 1960s were not unusual in this regard. Gang politics dominated much of Los Angeles. When asked to characterise the city's identity, Chuck Dizzle of Home Grown Radio paused briefly before saying, "We're survivors—in every sense of the word." From the Watts Rebellion to the Rodney King Uprising, from police brutality to gangbanging, Los Angeles' communities of colour have faced persistent threats. "There's families that actually feud because one's from one hood, one's from the other hood," according to Dizzle. "The way Los Angeles is organised, this is one hood, and this is another. You must live nicely together. You need to sort it out. Children from opposite sides of the rails attend school together. They attend primary school together, and when they step off the porch—that is, join a gang—they are forced to choose sides. We were homies. Now it's like, "Aaaah, those days are over." And imagine if my relative is slain and I find out it was done by folks in your neighbourhood."

Understanding the pervasiveness of gang culture provides new ideas on how to best approach young people growing up in that context. Influences such as "gangsta rap" are not causes, but rather effects.

"It's not like you wake up and say, 'Wow, that documentary inspired me.'" "I wanna go bang," Hussle stated. "Or, 'I heard this album.' Or, "I saw the video, and that's what I want to do." Not to suggest that's how other areas received it. Because there are many various reasons why people do what they do. But only as far as Los Angeles, the schoolteachers. It's the way of the street, period. "There's no alternative thing going on in the streets."

Creating alternatives to illegal hustling was a matter of survival, so when California voters approved Proposition 64, which legalised recreational marijuana usage in November 2016, Hussle and his team jumped right in. Legitimising the marijuana industry had advantages and disadvantages. People who had endangered their freedom by providing cannabis to the public when it was illegal had a difficult time transitioning onto the legal side of things. Hussle had a distinct advantage because of his celebrity. "I've got a built-in marketing mechanism by me being an artist with fans and with a platform," he elaborated to me. "So I didn't have the same obstacles that someone who was just hustling and carrying their packs would. It's similar to a liquor licence. There are just a limited number of licences available, and if you don't have a partner and can't obtain one on your own, you're barred from selling booze. Likewise with cannabis. If you don't have a partner, there is no need for him to partner with you; he will do it on his own."

According to accounts from the 1960s, there was an attempted burglary at the property in the fall of 2017. "Whoever it is, whatever it is, if you've got somebody doing something that you want to do, you might be envious of it," according to one of the performers. When Fatts and his colleagues investigated the attempted burglary, they wanted to determine whether the offender was acting alone or if the operation was planned. "They handled it like motherfuckers that were tutoring us would handle it," adds a member in their sixties. "They went out and did what they were supposed to do and that's what got 'em in the situation that brought all the attention to all of it."

A makeshift monument of blue candles quickly appeared on the pavement along the 5900 block of West Boulevard, along with blue and yellow flowers and Mylar balloons flapping in the breeze. Services for Stephen J. Donelson were held at Calvary Baptist

Church on Fairfax Avenue, immediately below Slauson.122 The thirty-year-old father cofounded and owned All Money In Records, The Marathon Clothing, and other businesses in the shopping plaza such as Wireless Connection and Baba Leo's Fish Shack, as well as Elite Human Hair, Fourth Ave Collective, and The Marathon OG, an exclusive strain developed by Hussle in collaboration with The Care Company. "You own 1/4 of everything I'm a part of," Hussle wrote on Instagram, accompanied by a shot of blue and yellow candles arranged to read FATTS. "I will make that worth 100 million before we meet again.

His emotions remained raw a few months later. Hussle became choked up near the end of his Rap Radar podcast interview when Elliott Wilson inquired about Fatts. "Man, that caught me completely off guard," Hussle stated. "I did not expect that at all. And the timing was insane. We've been sitting on everything. We've been holding back just to have everything done at once. We have all been looking forward to the opportunity to appreciate this moment. And it's a little fucked up—really fucked up—that my partner and homeboy aren't here to experience and profit from it. "And from like..." He cleared his throat and hesitated, brushing away a tear in his eye. "I don't want to go too deep into it. "I become emotional.

"I feel you," Wilson said. "Respect. Respect."

"But his kids, his kids would be proud of him."

Fatts is named as an executive producer on Victory Lap's credits, which is very appropriate. His services were vital to the overall success of the All Money In mission. Nonetheless, his death threw a veil over the team's huge win, making the announcement of the Atlantic Records collaboration in November 2017 somewhat bittersweet.

Hussle and his team ultimately revealed their multimillion-dollar joint venture arrangement with Atlantic Records in late November 2017. He had done his homework and put his trust in the management team, which included Craig Kallman and former Def Jam executives Julie Greenwald, Mike Kyser, and Kevin Liles, all of whom had remarkable track histories of establishing joint ventures such as Jay-Z's Roc-A-Fella histories and T.I.'s Grand Hustle.

Atlantic supported T.I. when he was imprisoned on federal weapons charges and later rocked with him as he rebuilt his career. "That's honourable," Hussle replied. "You don't see that." It didn't hurt that Hussle had known Dallas Martin, Atlantic's senior vice president of A&R, since 2011, when he worked with Rick Ross at Warner Music.

Despite living under the phrase "Fucc Tha Middleman" for years, Hussle did like the thought of collaborating with the renowned label that formerly housed Aretha Franklin and Ray Charles. Apparently, the feelings were mutual. "He's really looked up to," Kallman remarked. "I believe he is a true icon and culturally significant to the entire West Coast." I'm quite thrilled about the Victory Lap. I think you've crafted an amazing album, and I can't wait to get it out there."

Once Hussle agreed to work with Atlantic, everything began to move quickly. His crew sensed the shift immediately away. "He was just breaking down that wall of going to the real mainstream," DJ V.I.P. explains. "Not mainstream sellout, but just mainstream awareness." V.I.P., Hussle's official tour DJ, witnessed a five- to tenfold spike in attendance at his gigs. "Once that partnership evolved and started to grow, that's when we were doing bigger festivals," he told me. Hussle would soon be booked to appear on MTV's TRL and the BET Awards, as well as headline Broccoli Fest. "We had been at some of these shows before, on smaller stages," he recalled. "But not the prime-time slots."

Hussle did not dip his toe into the mainstream. He and the All Money In squad jumped in headfirst. Now that they were prepared, every door was open to them. They would soon form deals with Puma and Jay-Z's management agency, Roc Nation, putting things into high gear. "We had Jay right there," explains V.I.P. "Jay had never been so committed to a West Coast performer before. He was all hands on deck. He made his team and their assets completely available to us, and we were getting ready to begin employing them. That would have limited us to arenas. We would only have done large tours, whether co-headlining or headlining. They simply have the resources to book you in such large venues and sell out the seats."

Hustle and Boog attended the Lakers' game against the Minnesota Timberwolves at the Staples Center on Christmas Day in 2017. Hussle wore a Wilt Chamberlain throwback jersey and a pair of

Puma suedes in Lakers purple with gold stripes. Despite rookie Kyle Kuzma's 31 points, the Lakers fell 121-104, but Hussle triumphed. Just being courtside with his queen was a success. They'd been through a hard stretch during the last month. In late November, he tweeted about their decision to separate and focus on raising their children, then removed it. A few days later, his ex Tanisha, who still went by the name of Chyna Hussle on Twitter, posted something about how they never broke up. Social media may make life more confusing at times, especially when it comes to romantic relationships. However, reality inevitably returns at some point, and Hussle and Boog are soon back on track.

Their courtside flex at the Staples Center had the paparazzi going crazy, and Hussle's choice of footwear was another clever chess move, hinting at the Puma collaboration they would reveal on January 16, 2018. Hussle helped design the outfit, and the tracksuits looked formal on his six-foot three frame. Hussle donned the designs on stage and during interviews. Puma sponsored his events and donated thousands of dollars to help renovate the basketball court at 59th Street Elementary, which is across from his grandmother's home. Granny even got to drink champagne on the plane.

NBA All-Star Weekend is more like a week-long extravaganza with some of the world's highest-paid players balling out—in every meaning of the word. It was also an ideal setting for the Victory Lap rollout. All week, there was no doubt that Nipsey Hussle was the King of Los Angeles.

When rappers travel out of town, they frequently "check in" with a local gang for safety. Hussle referred to the technique as "friendly extortion," and stated that he prefers to move with respect. "When I come to Atlanta, I show respect and I tap in," according to him. "I am not in my hometown. I have my jewellery on. I could become a victim if I don't stroll and step carefully. As much as we secure, you are not bigger than the software."

On the evening of Tuesday, February 13—three days before the album's release—the same Brinks truck from the "Hussle & Motivate" video drove up in front of a Los Angeles strip club. The truck was now painted black and branded with All Money In logos. The back doors opened, and Adam, Cowboy, J Roc, Cobby, and

Nipsey Hussle leaped out, all dressed in AMI caps and black Victory Lap T-shirts and holding huge bundles of cash. "Neighbourhood!" they exclaimed.

Making the most of the circumstance, they launched a contest to win a 14-karat gold All Money In pendant. "Tha police buster ass towed our All Money In Brinks Truck," Hussle posted on Instagram, directing fans to drive up to the tow yard where the truck had been seized and take a photo with the hashtag #FREETHEBRINKSTRUCK. "We had a lot of people come down," stated the receptionist at Pepe's Towing on Boyle Avenue. "It was three hundred, four hundred niggas outside the gate takin' pictures," Hussle told me. "We didn't take things too seriously, though. "We laughed it off."

Hussle, J Stone, and BH partied in their city's streets the next night, dressed in a black durag, a white Puma Victory Lap tracksuit, and crazy gold chains. Despite the excitement surrounding Victory Lap's release, Hussle used the chance to speak out against the police. "One thing we don't respect is how the LAPD came through and took our Brink's truck," Hussle told the crowd. "We're putting on for the city and showing affection. We're raising the expectations of young niggas coming out of the hood. And we don't understand why the police want to hate on that. But, guess what? We're going to turn a negative into a good. So, the Brink's truck is back in Los Angeles. It is back in our hands. We're going all out this All-Star weekend. Victory Lap has been officially released.

The first time Ralo listened to the album in its entirety, he noticed something strange about the guest appearances. "Everybody's verse on Victory Lap was paying homage to Nipsey," the rapper claimed. Hip hop is a competitive sport. When one rapper is invited to rap on another rapper's song, there is always some subtle one-upmanship involved. Kendrick Lamar's song-stealing guest verse on Big Sean's "Control" is an extreme example. "It's an honour to see that type of shit," Ralo remarked. "To have a debut album out, with such high-profile features, and his peers praising him. That thing was nearly crazy. "As if they knew he'd die."

In between strip club celebrations and gold chain giveaways, Hustle took time to cut the ribbon on Vector90, the Crenshaw District coworking space, business incubator, and STEM academy he co founded. His business partner David Gross attended the inaugural event, as did L.A. City Councilmember Marqueece Harris-Dawson and Vector90 board member Don Peebles, a self-made Black tycoon with a $5 billion real estate portfolio. "He's building the tallest skyscraper on the West Coast right now," Hussle told the crowd. "And he is a first-generation success story." His father was a mechanic, and he achieved that level of achievement in one generation.

While Victory Lap hits like "Grinding All My Life" and "Hussle & Motivate" played in the background, invited guests and reporters explored the sleek venue, taking in information from an art show exposing the scarcity of Black talent at high-tech giants like Google and Facebook. Vector90 was created to help close the gap between South Central and Silicon Valley.

Later that night, Hussle was backstage at the Hollywood Palladium, where Rance and the 1500 or Nothin' band warmed up the stage. The formal Victory Lap release party was a star-studded affair. Hussle pulled out Marsha Ambrosius to sing the song "Real Big" alongside him. He invited Puffy out to perform "Young Niggas." He summoned Sacramento street legend Mozzy. He pulled out his day-one homeboy, J Stone. As a large screen projected the word VICTORY against a backdrop of red and blue, 1500 began playing the rhythm for "Last Time That I Checked" as Hussle introduced his daughter, Emani.

"That was my favourite guest of the night," Hustle explained. "She finished the set with me." Emani, dressed casually in a T-shirt and trousers, grabbed the microphone and rapped the chorus with impressive authority for a nine-year-old while her father's voice played in the background. Apparently, all those nights in the studio were not lost on her. Hussle wrapped his arm over his daughter's shoulders as she finished her bars, then carefully escorted her to the side of the stage as YG charged out, welcoming his homeboy with a tremendous pound that could be felt all the way back in the audience. Their spectacular performance ended the evening with a powerful statement of solidarity, leaving an unforgettable mark on L.A. rap history.

Hussle anticipated that the Victory Lap would mark the start of a new era in his career. "I've learned a lot just putting this out," he stated following the Victory Lap launch. "This is my first major label release. This is the first time I have mixed and mastered a project. It's the first time we've done a full campaign, marketed an album, ran radio ads, and so on. I felt like, "Cool, I got it." I figured it out. I understand the entire process. I know everyone at Atlantic. We have a working history. The next one has to be greater. It must continue to grow.

Nip, a hustler, wanted a platinum album so he could charge platinum pricing. But more than money, he desired respect as an artist and a man. "Nipsey Hussle is well-known," he explained. "They know he's from Los Angeles. He is respected in his city. He has made a few movements. However, in terms of music, I haven't been able to flex as much. And this record is an example of me moving in that direction. And I still have more room to improve and demonstrate what I am capable of."

Chapter 7: Too Big to Fail

London held thirty index cards, each written with a question intended to measure how well her beloved knew her. Unfazed by the pressure of being interrogated so intimately by his significant other—on camera, no less—Hussle accepted the challenge with a lighthearted competitive spirit. "See, he stays ready," Lauren explained with an endearing tone, "so he doesn't have to get ready."

"You got the script down!" Hussle responded, impressed. It should have been no surprise. This is what happens when you fall in love with an actress.

"This was a man who was proud to be with his woman," says Vanessa Satten, XXL's editor who featured Hussle on the cover in 2010. "You see a lot of rappers who are proud of how many ladies they have. Nipsey and Lauren's relationship appeared to be genuine love for each other, and the timing of their gorgeous fashion shoot together was particularly emotional."

The adorable eight-minute video, which was posted on March 28, 2019, a month after Hussle and Boog's epic GQ spread first published, has been viewed about 15 million times in the last year. It quickly became one of those moments that seemed meant to last forever, or at least as long as YouTube existed. Even if you know that the best love stories rarely end happily, there's an intoxicating delight in seeing two people bantering so flawlessly together.

"Where did we first meet?""My store is located on Crenshaw and Slauson.""What did I think of you?""She was absolutely ecstatic.

"I thought he was very tall."

"Career-wise, Nipsey Hussle and Lauren London occupy the same branch on the pop-culture tree," Mark Anthony Green said in his GQ feature of the duo. "I refer to this branch as The Branch White America Hasn't Exploited Yet. "It has advantages and disadvantages."

Hustle and David Gross called Vector90's STEM centre "Too Big to Fail," adopting a phrase popularised during the late-2000s financial crisis to justify government bailouts of failing Wall Street corporations with taxpayer money. According to Ben Bernanke, the chairman of the Federal Reserve, "a too-big-to-fail firm is one whose size, complexity, interconnectedness, and critical functions are such that, should the firm go unexpectedly into liquidation, the rest of the financial system and the economy would face severe adverse consequences." Hustle and Gross were implying that people can be as significant as financial organisations when they reclaimed the phrase and applied it to South Los Angeles locals. They had the hubris to claim that the individuals in this community, in particular, were too essential and interwoven to fail.

On Saturday, March 30, Hussle stopped by Puerto Nuevo Coffee on West Slauson for some green juice. He took Emani along because he was always looking for ways to spend more time with his family. "Do you know how kids spell love?" he often asked. "T-I-M-E." Finding personal time was a regular issue with studio sessions, video shoots, promotions, and his multiple enterprises. "That shit ain't easy," he explained. "But it's worth it because what you're doing is extending your stay here. You are extending your legacy. It's not going to be one-sided. "You get a reward out of that."

The Centinela Park Family is a Blood set from east Inglewood that shares territory with the Rollin' 60s. For decades, the competing sets have been sworn foes. Nipsey Hussle's song "Bullets Ain't Got No Names" tells the story of a time when he was on the field and his set went back-to-back against Centinela in one horrible night. "My hood is warring, so ain't no warnings," he rapped in a line that, like most of his music, is based on a true tale.

On March 30, 2019, the energy in Puerto Nuevo was entirely different. Nip and Firebugg had met in a neutral situation, perhaps by chance or fate—Nip with his kid and Firebugg with his fiancée. The stage was prepared for a strong convergence, a spontaneous gathering of minds.

Hussle's viewpoint had changed dramatically since his days of "putting in work" for the set, and Firebugg had gone through a similar shift. "Twelve years in prison instilled something in me," he told me. "Brought me up and awakened me as an adult man to understand the big picture. So, looking back, I realise that encounter was a blessing." He assumed he was just coming in for breakfast, but as he went into the restaurant, he recognized Hussle right away.

According to the old way of thinking, he caught Hussle ``slippin'' by walking up on him from behind. But Firebug wasn't feeling that vibe anymore.

"Any type of destructive, any type of violence, anything like that was never on my mind," he told me. Firebug had witnessed Nip's progress from behind bars, feeling proud that someone who had endured a similar lifestyle could improve himself, start enterprises, and give back to the community. "Off top, I'm looking at a man that came from the same blocks that I came from," he told me. "Different colour, different team, but transgressed to the point in the game where—I'm not even talking about millionaire status. I'm talking about the humanitarian on the block where we live. So when I walked up on him from behind, I was thinking, "Wow, that's Nip."

Hustle approached Firebug in the coffee shop booth, shook his hand, and spotted a tattoo on his arm. "Is that Malcolm?" he inquired. "Bro, I've been waiting on you." He firmly gripped Firebugg's hand.

"Bro, I had a vision, and I've been looking for a nigga with a voice and a solid mind," Hussle explained, recalling their last meeting. The year was 2007 and the location was Los Angeles Men's Central Jail. Hussle was on the run when he secured his recording contract, celebrated for a week in Jamaica before returning to Los Angeles to turn himself in. The first Bullets Ain't Got No Name mixtape was yet to be released. Tanisha Foster, his girlfriend, was pregnant with Emani. He had so much to live for, but on that particular day, everything was on the line.

"When I first fell, I was in the holding tank," Hustle explained, keeping his grip on Firebugg's hand. The Centinela Park Blood recalled him dimly. He'd seen a million people inside and experienced so much himself. "Nah," Hussle insisted. "You were in a holding tank. My homies had packed out one of your homies. "Your homie jumped my homie, so he jumped back." Although county jail inmates are normally divided by gang affiliation, when they initially arrive for processing, they are all grouped together in the "holding tank," where anything can happen. Fights are not unusual. Sometimes these conflicts are fatal, resulting in an inmate's body being "packed out." Firebug was beginning to remember. The younger Crips were outnumbered. They wouldn't have a chance.

What was the point? In that moment, he had the authority to stop the onslaught, and he utilised it.

"We came in and you told your homies, 'Nah, we ain't about to jump on them,'" Hussle replied. "I never forgot that, bro."

"He never let my hand go," Firebug recounted. "And he just took me on a whole journey." They discussed the drive-bys that inspired the song "Bullets Ain't Got No Names." Hussle told him he remembered being on the block with the homies and hearing them say, "Watch that corner." They'd had enough time to giggle over the memories by now.

They never mentioned a "peace treaty," because that had been done before. Gang treaties never seemed to last. Whether the cops violated the truce or someone else did something to someone, the strain always built up and the drama began all over again. The solution was not another treaty, but ownership and economic empowerment. Rick Ross used the phrase "buying back the block" in a song featuring Hussle on the "Refinance Version" remix. "Operation buy back the 60s," Nip said, before outside forces could "gentrify the whole inner city, genocide the whole inner city."

Hussle felt comfortable walking up to Slauson and seeing the businesses he and his brother had started, knowing that they had provided work for people in the community. He was now sketching out a plan to create South L.A. that was larger than Hyde Park. "I'm tryin' to do that all the way to the beach," he said. "But between me and the beach is Inglewood..." I've been waiting for someone to tell you. "Who else will tell the story better than you?"

The popular coffee shop was now quiet. It seemed like everyone was leaning toward their booth to hear the conversation. "We both acknowledged that we were sworn enemies by gang rights, but we said we were born brothers by essence," Firebug wrote in an Instagram image featuring the two of them together. Hussle instructed him, "Let's get this flick and fuck the streets up," before he and Emani returned outside. "I felt like I just witnessed two kings at a sit-down," Firebug's girlfriend added later.

"When you cross paths with another actual individual," Firebug remarked after their meeting, "the expression 'peace treaty' will never come up. Because we already know what level we are in the game. When you go further, a prophet recognizes another prophet. When he saw Malcolm on my arm, he grabbed Malcolm's chain. I just think about it in retrospect. It didn't hit me till later.

Hustle informed Killa Twan about his meeting with Firebug shortly after it occurred. Hussle's boyhood pal was raised in a Blood area, thus he and Nip had been crossing gang lines for years. Twan recognized the significance of what had happened. "These two have fought each other before," Twan told me. "They've shot at each other before..." If it was another weak person, the situation would be dire. But because he is such a powerful man, they were able to sit and talk, eat, and communicate as men, rather than as Inglewood Blood and Crenshaw Crip.``

Angelique Smith couldn't sleep well. After tossing and turning till the early morning, Ermias Asghedom's mother fell asleep just before sunrise on Sunday, March 31, about 6 a.m. She was a deeply spiritual person who attended the KRST Unity Center of AfRaKan Spiritual Science on a regular basis. She lived her life by the premise that "everything is in the divine perfect order of our Creator." Angelique has always had a very deep bond with her son Ermias, who was born on her birthday. For the previous two weeks, she had an unshakeable feeling that something wasn't right.

Hussle was not meant to be at the Marathon Clothing store on Sunday afternoon, March 31. He didn't have a particular schedule, although he usually stopped by on weekday mornings after dropping Emani off at school. Unless there was a public event planned, J Roc, his security, rarely accompanied him—especially on Sundays.

"Always by himself," said Cowboy, also known as Big Thundercat, the man who collaborated with Hussle and sponsored Lil Thundercat's hood show in the mid-2000s. He was now employed full-time at the shopping complex. "Only time he ever really had security is when he was on the road or on tour," Cowboy told me. "As far as being in the inner city or coming to the job, he never had security ever."

This particular Sunday was memorable for several reasons. Hussle had been out late the night before to celebrate his godbrother Adam's

"C-day" at midnight. Their business associate Jorge Peniche refers to "Dammy Dam" Andebrhan as "one of the guys that helped shape a lot of the sonics of the Nipsey Hussle brand and music." Hussle shared a photo on Instagram of him and Adam dressed in white with gold chains, looking strong and prosperous. Hussle saluted him in the post, writing, "Day 1 with this all $ In Shit!" Adam, like Hussle, had grown up with Fatts, and they had both made it a point to care for his family after his death a year and a half ago.

Nip drove to Anaheim on Saturday evening to witness the Texas Tech Red Raiders defeat the Gonzaga Bulldogs and advance to the Final Four of the NCAA Men's Basketball Tournament. Hussle couldn't miss this game, even though it meant driving through rush hour traffic for hours. He'd been invited by his old buddy and mentor Big Bob Francis, who handed him the books Contagious, which inspired Hussle's Proud2Pay act, and The 22 Immutable Laws of Branding, which urged him to see himself as a brand rather than merely an artist. Big Bob's son, Brandone Francis, a second-string forward for Texas Tech, had told his buddies that his favourite rapper would be in the arena, and Hussle arrived just in time to witness him come off the bench and shoot a three-pointer. Brandone finished the game with six points, which was exactly enough to give his team the win. Hussle cheered as loudly as anyone else at the Honda Center. "He's always going to be my big brother," Brandone remarked. "I'm excited that he was part of the historic moment that we had as a team."

Hussle's fortuitous encounter with Firebug the day before sent Nip's head spinning with thoughts. They had been texting one other since he left the coffee shop. Firebug had lost one of his closest friends during Centinela's struggle with the 60s. Putting his pain aside and embracing the vision of oneness was a significant step forward.

On Monday, April 1, Hussle was slated to attend a meeting organised by Roc Nation with Los Angeles Police Commissioner Steve Soboroff (also a rich real estate developer who built Staples Center) and LAPD Chief Michel R. Moore. "Our goal is to work with the department," according to the letter from Roc Nation, "to help improve communication, relationships, and work towards changing the culture and dialog between LAPD and the inner city." Hussle was suspicious after years of police harassment, but he tried to be open-minded. The police were going to be either part of the answer or part of the problem, but it was worth a shot.

On his journey down Slauson toward The Marathon Clothing flagship shop that Sunday, he passed by the corner of Crenshaw, where construction teams were building on the new light rail line that would transport travellers from LAX to the storied neighbourhood where Hussle had established his claim. Nip collaborated with Councilmember Marqueece Harris-Dawson to create the Destination Crenshaw concept, which was intended to be both a cultural festival and a barrier against gentrification. The multimillion-dollar project brings together local artists, curators, and Zena Howard, a Black architect from Perkins & Will, the firm that designed the Smithsonian National Museum of African American History and Culture. Hussle was actively involved in the planning of the 1.3-mile "unapologetically Black" open-air museum, which would record the history of African Americans in Los Angeles. Thanks to the community art initiative, commuters travelling the Metro rail, no matter who they are or where they are going, will be immersed in the story of Black people in Los Angeles as they travel through the Crenshaw District.

These and countless other ideas raced through Hussle's mind at 2:53 p.m., when he drove up to the Marathon shop in his black Maybach with All Money In insignia embossed and embroidered across the interior.

Hussle tweeted a cryptic tweet while seated in the parking lot: "Having strong enemies is a blessing." He understood that most of his followers would miss the disguised reference to Firebugg, but as with so much of Hussle's life and work, those who were aware would know. He could not have predicted the events that occurred over the next twenty-nine minutes.

"Sam was with Granny at the crib," adds V.I.P., who was in North Carolina at the time for a private session. "Nip was simply stopping by the store to help the homie acquire some clothes. "He just pulled up to look for someone from the neighbourhood who had just gotten out—and shit happened."

Kerry Louis Lathan Sr., also known as Cousin Kerry, was fifty-six years old. He was born in Houston, migrated to Los Angeles as a child, and became a member of the Rolling 60s. He had previously been convicted of four felony drug crimes before being sentenced to prison for murder in 1996. Though Hussle didn't know Kerry—he was just eleven years old when he was locked up—shortly after he returned home on parole, Nipsey sent him a care box of Marathon gear as a gesture of goodwill "on hood." Kerry was trying to rebuild his life, reunite his family, and acclimate to a completely new world. That day, he mentioned he needed some garments to comfort a friend who had recently lost their father. "My nephew was complaining that I'm not in prison anymore so I don't have to wear the same shirt," he responded. "'You're free.'"

While waiting for Cousin Kerry, Hussle signed autographs, took photographs with clients at The Marathon Clothing store, and spoke with Cowboy and Rimpau, his old classmate and lifelong musical partner. "I was just telling him how proud I was of him," Cowboy explained afterward. "It felt like the old times again, just talking and reminiscing."

Born Eric Ronald Holder Jr., the man Hussle knew as Shitty Cuz was a Rollin' 60s member and wannabe rapper who recorded under the name Fly Mac. Hussle's estate refuted rumours that he was formerly signed to All Money In, and few of his close circle recall him at all.

According to his SoundCloud page, Shitty Cuz was neither creative nor focused, uploading only five mediocre tracks over a four-year period. Nonetheless, Fly Mac included the tagline "plenty niggas hate cuz I'm da great" on his 2015 SoundCloud profile. Hustle has long referred to himself as "The Great" in both real life and on Twitter. Hussle, on the other hand, backed up his boasts of grandeur with appealing lyrics, a distinct voice, a sense of flow and melody, charm, integrity, and determination—all of which are lacking in the few Fly Mac tracks available online. Holder, who was only four years younger than Nip, failed to reach even a quarter of Nipsey Hussle's rap career success.

Holder exited the van and proceeded into Master Burger to purchase some chilli cheese fries, then strolled over to The Marathon Clothing store, where Hussle, Cowboy, and Rimpau were standing together.

Holder was shirtless with a black bandanna tied over his neck, showing off his gang tattoos—H60D CRIP at the top of his chest and SIXTIES across his stomach.

In this sense, "paperwork" refers to court documents that indicate someone in police custody reached an agreement to minimise their penalty. In other words, the documentation would identify him as a "snitch." In street culture, where loyalty is paramount and snitching might mean life or death, "paperwork" is treated very seriously. It is downloaded, printed, handed about, tampered with, and quietly discussed. The consequences for untidy paperwork can be harsh, often resulting in a "DP," which stands for disciplinary punishment—a beating or worse.

Around that time, the woman who had driven Holder to the shopping plaza exited her Cruze and approached the group of men, intending to take a selfie with Nip. The woman's identity has not been revealed since she later became a snitch, negotiating a deal with the Los Angeles County district attorney to testify against Holder. She is named in court transcripts as. Under the terms of her deal with the DA, the driver was immune from prosecution for anything she said on the witness stand, as long as her testimony was completely honest. If she was caught lying about anything under oath, she may still face prosecution.

Cowboy described the temperature of their conversation differently. "There was no hint of any animosity," he told me. "If they had any words, I would have escorted him out. Had they had any kind of argument... Nipsey was basically watching out for him, telling him, 'I haven't read it, I don't know if it's true or not, but you need to handle it.' That's exactly what Nipsey was doing."

Holder's talk with Hussle lasted about four minutes and fifteen seconds, according to time codes obtained from several security cameras throughout the shopping plaza. Shitty mentioned his music toward the end of their conversation, according to Cowboy.

"He asked if we had heard his rap," Cowboy recounted. "He replied, 'Yeah, I've been in the studio. "I finished my new song."He asked if we had heard it, and we said, 'Nah, we haven't heard your song,' or anything." Then Shitty went away and returned to Master Burger.

Standing alongside parked automobiles in front of The Marathon Clothing entrance, the Grammy-nominated rapper continued to converse with star-struck customers and sign their merchandise. "He was taking photographs with a little baby," Kerry said in an interview. "His mother requested a selfie with her son. He was going to turn three the next day.

Eric Holder walked out of the Master Burger and told Witness #1 that he needed two dollars to pay for his meal. She gave him a five, and he completed the chilli cheese fries deal. Then he returned to where Hussle was standing.

"I want to call your attention now back to the top of the video at the Master Burger door," Deputy District Attorney John McKinney told Herman ``Cowboy'' Douglas as he sat on the witness stand during grand jury proceedings on May 6, 2019. "Holder appears to approach your group again. Do you notice this? He appears to shake Trump's hand or dap him up, implying he is giving him a pound. He then rushes back toward the white automobile, holding something in his hands. "Is that what the video shows?"

"Yes," Cowboy responded.

"Do you recall that happening?"

"No."

When Holder returned to the car, he informed Witness #1 that he wanted to consume his lunch. "Not right here," she said, according to her grand jury evidence. "Well, we could just drive around," she answers, responding to his suggestion. She pulled out of the parking lot and turned right onto Slauson.

During Cowboy's grand jury testimony, McKinney, a young Black prosecutor from the Major Crimes Division of the Los Angeles County District Attorney's Office, inquired as to whether there was anything about Holder that made Cowboy wish to separate Nipsey from him. "I felt something in my gut," he added. "At that moment, I questioned why I was feeling this way..." Just being in his presence made me anxious, as did his behaviour and what he was saying.

Cowboy repeatedly referred to Holder's attack as "a straight snake move" on the witness stand and in different on-camera interviews, casting doubt on his own decision to take a lunch break at the exact moment he selected. "I just replay it over and over," he told the television program Extra. "I wish I had done things differently. I wish I would never have left his side. There was never any drama, no disagreement, and no dispute. It was nothing. It was an all-out, sly snake manoeuvre."

Rimpau did not testify before the grand jury and has not given any interviews regarding what happened that day. "I beat myself up about March 31st every day. I want to do something, but there's nothing I can do to bring you back," he wrote on Instagram on April 26. "I just want to shyne with you one more time. Brodee I worked so hard to get my shyt together, bro, and I'm delighted you saw my progress. I thank you for pushing me and instilling discipline in me. He closed his message with the phrase "LLKingNH," which stands for "Long live King Nipsey Hussle."

After leaving the parking lot, Witness #1 drove around the block in her Cruze, turning right on Crenshaw and right again on Fifty-Eighth Place. They took another right into an unmarked alleyway between Crenshaw and West Boulevard, which divides the shopping plaza from the Shell gas station on the corner. Witness #1 claims she initially noticed the gun, a black 9mm pistol.

"As we are driving he's pulling out the gun," she told the jury. "I saw him loading the bullets into the magazine… kind of holding it towards the window but not, and I was just like, 'You're not gonna do a drive-by in my car.'"

The district attorney inquired as to where he obtained the rifle. "He pulled it out so fast I don't know where he got it from," she told me. She had not observed the semiautomatic handgun earlier that day, when she picked him up shirtless in a small town for a half-hour drive to Los Angeles.

In prior evidence, the driver stated that she had seen him carrying a similar gun for the preceding month, which he claimed he needed "for protection."

She said he frequently tucked it into his waistband. She also claimed to be unaware that he was a gang member, despite the obvious tattoos all over his upper body.

"Did he say anything to you about Nipsey Hussle?" DA McKinney asked. "Did he seem angry with anybody?"

"No," she responded. "It seemed like his normal self to me."

"Okay," the DA said, emphasising his point. "Why did you think at that moment that he was gonna use the gun to shoot somebody?"

She claimed she had never seen him load the gun before. "Every time he is with me he will just have it on him," she told me. "I never saw him mending or putting items in there. I never saw him play with it. As if he is about to use it.

Witness #1 claims that when she told Holder she would not allow any drive-by shootings in her car, Holder put the pistol away. The DA did not pursue her further on why she would consider a drive-by. In her initial interview with officers from the Seventy-Seventh Division, she reportedly stated that Holder wanted her to drive him around the block so he could perform a drive-by. She then claimed that the officers' questioning had confused her throughout her five-hour interrogation.

As they circled the block again, Holder directed her to pull up on West Fifty-Eighth Place in the parking lot behind Fatburger, where all of the staff uniforms are co branded with The Marathon Clothing's signature Crenshaw logo. "Pull over in here," he said. "I want to eat." The front of her car faced the alley leading to the shopping complex.

He slipped on a crimson T-shirt while eating some chilli cheese fries. Witness #1 stated that she inquired whether Holder was ready to leave yet.

Something in her testimony did not make sense. McKinney questioned Witness #1 again: "You didn't ask him, 'Why did you bring a pistol in my car? I might get in trouble for this if we get stopped. "Anything like that?"

"No," she replied. "I simply wasn't thinking about it..." I asked if he was ready to go and began moving my car towards the alley. And then he said, 'Wait. Do not go anywhere. "I'll be back."

"All right," she says she told him. "Hurry up."

Many aspects of Witness #1's testimony seemed to require a suspension of disbelief. The prosecutor needed her to make the murder case credible, but some of her responses appeared strained. "Didn't you wonder, 'What is he talking about?'" McKinney asked. "'Where is he going?'"

Once again, the motorist ignored what appeared to be clear, logical solutions. "No," she replied. "I simply assumed he was going to go get something or whatever. Perhaps he forgot something or wanted to get something.

"What direction did he go in?"

She stated that he went down the alley, "towards Slauson Way."

"Did you see him with the gun at any time?"

"No," she replied. Witness #1 stated that he was merely carrying a takeout container of chilli cheese fries. As he walked through the lane toward Slauson, he placed the container on the bonnet of a parked white truck, she explained. Then he turned the corner toward Master Burger, returning to the parking lot where he last saw Nipsey.

Meanwhile, in front of the Marathon store, Hussle was still conversing with fans, and Cousin Kerry had made no headway toward obtaining the new shirt that was supposed to be the main reason Nipsey came out on a Sunday.

"Yo, Nipsey man," Kid Flashy told him. "I'm here for a BMF audition with 50 Cent. Do you mind if I take a picture with you and post it?

"Yes, no problem," he replied. "Come on."

Soon after taking his shots, Kid Flashy observed someone approaching. "The kid came back around the corner," Flashy explains. "I passed straight past him, and I had a feeling something was amiss. But I couldn't exactly pinpoint it. Then I saw him pull out and begin hitting him."

When cousin Kerry and Nipsey Hussle were standing face to face between two parked automobiles, chaos ensued. "A guy just came around shooting," Kerry remarked. Kerry told the grand jury that just before the rounds were fired, the gunman spoke with Hussle. "I believe he said, 'You're through.'"

In the intensity of the moment, Kerry didn't notice the gunman's face. "The first thing I saw was gunfire," he claimed. "I looked up and saw him shoot, and that was it. I saw a flash... When you see a shooting at one o'clock in the afternoon, you're too close to the gun. "So I ran."

Holder approached Hussle, his arms fully extended. In his right hand, he held a silver revolver, and in his left, a black semi automatic, both firing at close range. One of the first shots struck Kerry in the back, right below his waist, and chipped a chunk of bone off his pelvis. "When I turned to run, it knocked my legs from up under me," he told me. "It was hot." "Fire is hot." He landed face down on the pavement. "I was moving my feet to see if my legs still worked."

Hussle collapsed shortly after. Kerry could see part of his body lying on the ground beyond the automobile tire that was blocking his eyesight. He overheard the guy fire. He heard ladies scream.

DA McKinney inquired about the firing pattern, which was either continuous or staccato.

"It was like one, two, three, and then it stopped," Kerry explained. "Then it came back—one, two, three more—and stopped. Then it came back. I was like, 'I'm sure this guy's gonna finish me off because I can't move.' But he didn't." Holder fired ten shots in three bursts of gunfire.

Kerry overheard Hussle saying three words to Shitty Cuz: "You got me."

Then Shitty came up to Hussle and kicked him once in the head before fleeing.

Cowboy was eating his fajita bowl in the Marathon store break room when he heard a gunshot. "I heard maybe a few gunshots," he added. "I started running to the front. I heard several more gunshots." He rushed through the front door, just in time to see Holder racing around the corner and Nipsey laying on the floor.

Aside from Hustle and Kerry, Shermi Villanueva was also injured by a bullet. Fortunately, the shot struck his belt buckle, leaving him startled but uninjured. "Who did this to you?" someone said to Hussle. Kerry heard him speak a name but couldn't understand it.

Witness #1 was sitting in her car with the engine running and perusing social media on her phone when she heard the bullets. She couldn't see the plaza from where she was parked, but she noticed a man sprinting in that direction. "I was just like, 'Oh my God,'" she remembered. " 'What's happening? I hope you're fine. You should hurry up!

"Let me get out of here" was the first thing that sprang to mind. However, she didn't. "I didn't know if he got hurt or if something happened," she told the judge. "So I waited on him."

District Attorney McKinney posed the obvious question. "Did it cross your mind that the gunshots you heard were fired by him?" Once again, she said no.

Then she noticed Holder rushing up the alleyway. "What's going on?" she inquired as soon as he entered the car. "Drive," he replied. "Drive before I slap you." He had never spoken to her like that before. "What's going on?" she asked. "You talk too much," was his response.

"I just kept driving," witness #1 stated. "I didn't want him to hit me or nothing like that."

Although security camera footage retrieved by LAPD officers showed Holder with one gun in each hand, the driver claims she saw nothing until he got into the car. "He had a revolver on this side," she told me. "Like he didn't want me to see it." He hid the pistol in the bag that his chilli cheese fries had come in.

"You knew something bad happened in that parking lot at that point, didn't you?" said the deputy attorney general. "What did you think happened in the plaza parking lot?"

"I just felt like I knew there was shooting going on," she informed me. "I was unsure if he was the shooter. I was not sure if he was being shot at. "I just knew something had happened."

Sam answered the phone when it rang at Granny's place. "He got the call and ran out of here so fast," Margaret Boutte recalled. "He never does that." When he departed, she took up the phone and called her daughter. "Angel, something must have happened," she said to me. "Samiel jumped up. He did not take his shower. "He got out of here so quickly." Sam pressed the accelerator and sped down Slauson, running red lights all the way to Crenshaw.

"I ran over to Nip and held him," Cowboy added. "He had a pulse, and he went in and out of consciousness. But he fought, and fought hard. There were red stains on his T-shirt. Cowboy applied pressure with his palms to stem the bleeding. "He was still breathing, chewing his tongue a little bit," Cowboy recounts. "If his eyes began to roll back a little bit, I said, 'Nip, wake up!' "And he'd snap out of it." Cowboy's options were limited to praying and waiting for paramedics.

Blacc Sam got there first. He had been afraid about something like this happening to his younger brother for years. "There's no reason for him to still be alive," he told himself as he noticed bullet wounds in Nipsey's knee, stomach, and under his left armpit. Sam attempted to tune out the turmoil around him by carefully listening to the 911 operator and counting chest compressions.

"Nip is sporadic," Sam subsequently said to the Los Angeles Times. "Nip is going to pull up and hop out of the Jordan Downs projects, Nickerson Gardens, or any 'ghetto in L.ACompton, or Watts—solo with $150,000 in jewellery around his neck and a $80,000 Rolex without any protection. That's why people adored him."

When the paramedics arrived, Sam let them take charge. The EMS team attempted to stabilise Hussle by administering an IV and a breathing tube. They didn't discover the wound on his head until they placed him onto a stretcher.

Killa Twan remained cool when he heard Nip had been shot. He'd just hung off the phone with Hussle an hour and a half ago. Twan had gone to The Marathon Clothing store to get shirts and socks and had just missed him. "There's so much we've been through," he told himself. "He's all right."

Then someone showed him an Instagram Live post and said, "Nah, bro, you need to go check." He hurried from Watts to Crenshaw, arriving just as his friend was about to be taken to the hospital.

Twain's cousin, who lived nearby, grabbed him and said, "Bro, you don't wanna see."

"Huh?" he exclaimed in surprise. "But he's gonna be alright though, right?"

His cousin shook his head gently. "Nah, bro gone."

"Are you sure?" Twan asked.

"Man, we know," his cousin responded. "We've seen that shit too many times. We've seen too many lifeless bodies. Fuck what they're talking about. He's already gone.

Twan caught sight of the paramedics bringing Nipsey away. "I remember the white turban he had on his head," he tells me. "I noticed how red his face was as they loaded him into the ambulance. "I said, 'Hell nah.'"

When Angelique Smith arrived at the shopping complex, her son had already been whisked away in an ambulance. "What happened?" she asked a police officer on the spot.

"Someone was shot," the officer responded.

"Who?" she inquired.

"Nipsey Hussle."

"My spirit said, 'Oh, oh. That is it. That is why," she said during a memorial service at the BET Awards. "I finished processing my son's assassination." Her choice of words, "assassination," rather than "death" or "murder," was remarkable.

She soon bumped across Rimpau, who had fled the area when the bullets were fired and returned to the retail mall, visibly terrified. She placed her hands on his shoulders and attempted to contact her son's friend. "Look into my eyes, Evan," she stated. "You understand that we are spiritual beings enjoying a physical experience, Evan? Do you comprehend that? So, even though our bodies "die" on this side of eternity, our spirits continue to live. We emerge from this vessel and move on." She sensed a spirit of retribution and vengeance enveloping him. "I don't even know what words I used because I was very frightened then," she said. But at the end, she thought she had "chased those spirits away from him."

YG was in DJ Mustard's house, watching March Madness on television. Michigan State and Duke competed for a chance to meet Texas Tech in the Final Four. YG placed a bet on the game with Ty Dolla $ign. Jade, his "day-one homegirl" who worked at the Marathon shop, contacted to say she had heard about Nipsey's shooting. While YG was telling Mustard the news, she called back to confirm that he had been shot four times. YG got into his pickup and inquired as to which hospital he would be transported to.

"She called back and said something else. I just got up and left. I went to pick up my truck. I got in the truck and I'm leaving. I'm like, 'Where are you going? Like, where is bro going? So I passed by Mustard's place, and he had gotten into his automobile. He was like, 'Shit, I thought you went already.' I said, 'Nah, hop in my stuff.' So we all jumped into my pickup. And they told us where they were taking Bro. And we were on our way, perhaps 15 or 20 minutes away. And they're like, 'Homie ain't making it.' "

Chapter 8: Higher and Higher

Seattle-based hair stylist Tatum Herman was Hussle's favourite barber and braider. "She is the truth," he used to say. He would take her on tour with him whenever she was available, although she didn't particularly enjoy life on the road.

When Herman was asked to braid Nipsey's hair for the wake, she was a little scared. "I brought his favourite tea," she recalled, "so that the whole room could smell aromatic. I brought a few crystals, some sage, and palo santo. It was a ritual, because I knew I had to be in a certain space." She thought it would be harder that day, but she felt his presence in the room.

"Nip was very tender-headed," she said. "I mean, he would be moving around and he could not handle it. When I did the first braid, I swear to God I heard him say, 'T, this the first time it doesn't hurt.' His spirit was there with me."

Herman was not the only one who felt Hussle's presence that day. Inside the Staples Center, Lauren's nine-year-old son, Kameron Carter, spoke to the capacity crowd. "On the night of April second I had a dream," he said. "I was in paradise and I was playing in the ocean water when Ermias popped up right behind me. He said, 'What up, Killa?' 'Cause that's my nickname to him. I turned around and I yelled his name and I gave him a hug. Shortly, he was gone but it was still cool I guess."

Dressed in a tie and jacket with an image of Hustle on his lapel, Kameron recalled telling his mom about the dream. "After I told her I was thinking about it and I realised that Ermias told me what heaven was like. He told me it was paradise."

Kameron shared a memory of his stepfather standing at the window in the morning and saying "Respect" each day. "So on the count of three I want everybody to yell RESPECT," he told the auditorium, and then began counting down. "Three, two, one..." On his command, twenty-one thousand voices spoke as one. "Respect!"

"In memory of Ermias Asghedom," Kameron said in closing. "August 15, 1985, to 2019 March 31st."

"I was front row," says Killa Twan of the memorial service. "That was epic. That was amazing. That was something I will never forget. As many times as he talked about selling out the Staples Center, I didn't think it would be that way. That shit was sold out."

"He packed out Staples Center at a funeral," said Wack 100, manager of Blueface and The Game, in a controversial No Jumper interview months later. "But have you seen Nipsey Hussle headlining Staples Center and his fans being true fans, come out and pack it out for him? I saw Kendrick Lamar sell it out three nights in a row. We just talkin' numbers. We're not talking' personal opinions." In Wack's opinion, Hussle was not worthy of "legend" status because his career had not yet reached that point at the time of his death. "Is it fucked up it happened?" Wack said. "Definitely fucked up it happened. Do I wish we could rewind life and he can re-do it again? Definitely. Did hip hop take a loss? Definitely." Still Wack insisted that Hussle did not deserve to be called a legend. "We didn't lose a legend at the time because the fans and the radio and things like that didn't support him to get him to where he shoulda been. Would he eventually get there? I believe so. Was he that what they say he is at the time of his demise? Definitely not. And we're just talking numbers." Hussle's bodyguard J Roc didn't appreciate Wack's opinion and later punched him in the face backstage at Rolling Loud.

Smoke DZA and Jonny Shipes were among those who paid their respects at the Staples Center. "His service was so hard to articulate," says DZA. "It wasn't even a regular service. We were all mourning. It was a show, it was a nightclub, the NBA finals. It was everything as far as the people in there. I'm sure it's some shit that he's probably laughing about. You've got LeBron, you've got Kendrick Lamar. It was the Who's Who... All of these people honoured him inside the Staples Center. The only other person who had a funeral in the Staples Center was Michael Jackson," DZA said with a laugh. "You feel me? So that's just the magnitude my man was on."

The words that Nip appreciated, his brother said, were the words of encouragement. "Whether he said it or not," Sam said, "the pats on the back, it meant a lot to him. 'Bro, keep doin' your thing.' 'We appreciate what you're doing.' 'You're making it look good.' You're putting us on the map.' That shit meant a lot to him. And that shit meant a lot to me from everybody who did that."

Quoting a lyric from Hussle's song "I Don't Stress," Sam said, "If I die today I made the set proud, nigga." Fighting to control his emotions, Sam spoke to his brother as the Staples Center filled with thunderous applause. "You made the world proud! You know? Look at this shit, bro!"

There is no doubt that Hussle's legacy has made the world proud. His face, depicted in murals throughout the city, is now recognized all over the planet. His love of books—and the reading lists he would share with friends—inspired book clubs to form, gathering people together in his name to read and discuss Hussle's favourite works.

After gathering himself for a moment, Sam continued. "A lot of people thought, comin' up, and when he first got signed, he was gonna get some money and leave. Like he said, they didn't have a fuckin' clue. They had no clue of what he really was gone' do. I want everybody to know, Nip…" Sam paused for a long time "his heart and soul on Crenshaw and Slauson."

Samiel and Ermias Asghedom were as close as two brothers could be. They spoke to each other about everything, including death. "We used to talk." Sam said. "We gotta go. We don't know if we're gonna go at eighty, sixty, thirty, or twenty. But the one thing is to make sure when you go, you go the right way. You stand up for what you believe in. You put your money where your mouth is. You never fold. Never let the pressure sway you from doing' what you wanna do. Never let anything, the politics, stop you from coming around and staying around. And I hope everybody knows that that's what bro did. Bro stayed and he died on Crenshaw and Slauson. And everybody who showed love, even the ones who didn't, Nip had nothin' but love. Nothin' but love and respect and humbleness."

In his song "Ocean Views," Hussle asked for a Stevie Wonder song to be played at his funeral. At the Staples Center on April 11, 2019, Wonder came to sing in person. But first he had something to say. "I knew him from hearing his music," said the R&B icon, "hearing him rap, and had the pleasure through someone who's very close to my wife—Pastor P—who arranged a meeting for myself to have a meeting with him for us to talk. I was able to meet him as well as Lauren. We were celebrating Pastor P's birthday. But as well, celebrating the fact that we had a good conversation and looked forward to a wonderful life.

"It is a heartbreak to again lose a member of our family," Stevie continued. "It is a heartbreak because it's so unnecessary. We, to be a civilised nation, a civilised world... We still are living in a time where ego, anger, and jealousy are controlling our lives. It is so painful to know that we don't have enough people taking a position that says, 'Listen, we must have stronger gun laws.' " The Staples Center cheered his words, too late to make a difference for Hussle. Still, they cheered.

Even after Stevie's last song was sung, there were still more stories to be told, more tears to be shed. The faithful filed out of the Staples Center into late afternoon sunshine. Tens of thousands of mourners filled the streets of Los Angeles, on foot, on motorcycles and ATVs, on horseback, children on their mothers' shoulders. They climbed up lampposts and perched on rooftops to get a view as the king of L.A. passed by. Helicopters hovered overhead. Marching bands made a joyful noise, and everywhere, from every corner, the voice of Nip Hussle the Great rang out, echoing through his domain. Hussle's pallbearers—family and the closest of homies—wore white gloves as they lifted his casket into a silver hearse with an Eritrean flag on the roof and took him for one last ride through his city—every set, every hood. Everywhere they went, well-wishers turned out to pay their respects as his procession rolled through the streets of L.A., flanked by motorcycles and adoring crowds all along the twenty-five-mile route.

"It was Bloods, Crips, Hispanic, Asian—I don't care what," said Cowboy. "Every hood we rolled through, the whole city showed love. We rolled all the way to Watts, came all the way back to Slauson and Crenshaw."

"I want to salute the L.A. police," said Steve Lobel. "Throughout the parade and all of the stuff at his shop and everything, they didn't come in forcefully and tell people to leave and this and that. They fell back and let it go. I've seen things where riots start because the police get overprotective or say, 'Hey, get out of here.' And this was amazing, just to see the helicopters and the drones and all this stuff. It was crazy and he was going through all the enemy hoods and they were just loving him. He broke a lot of barriers. So, God might have needed him."

Dexter Browne was in Trinidad with his family when the memorial took place, mourning the complex, charismatic young man he had raised like a son. "That really hurt us to lose him," he said. "It really took a toll on us. And it was hurtful not having an opportunity to attend the funeral given our history." The grand memorial reminded Dexter of all the funerals that Hussle paid for. "When he got on and he started making money, his allegiance to the hood never wavered," says Dexter. "For the homies who got shot and stuff like that, he would pay for the funerals and that obviously would give him some power over time. He became what he wanted to become. I don't think he wanted to lose his life for it, but oftentimes you don't get to pick exactly how it happens if you dream for it."

After the memorial Atlantic Records approached Jorge Peniche about designing billboards in Hussle's honour. "Man, we gotta do this," they told him, "because the city and the people are hurting like they lost a family member." If the city was hurting, Hussle's actual family was heartbroken. "The people who knew him very well were completely devastated, broken into a million pieces," Peniche said. He hoped that the image might be part of the healing process. He got to work with the intention of "reinvigorating the spirit of resiliency and also celebrating the legacy and the greatness and the legend of Nip Hussle."

"We had to do it," Peniche said. "We had to run a billboard that represented that." The design was finalised on the day his wife, the on-air personality Letty Peniche, was giving birth to the couple's second son. "We were in the delivery room," Peniche remembered. "My wife had just gotten there. We had just gotten settled in. The only creative thing is I got the photo and we were just trying to figure out how to design it."

The image was a shot from the "Higher" video set, taken by Roc Nation exec Lenny S. "Sam threw out the term 'Prolific,' which is something that was synonymous with Nipsey's name at this point," Peniche said. "Something that he took ownership of and had a licence of. And I said, 'Okay, Prolific. This is great.' " So there he sat with his laptop, in the delivery room, still mourning himself, and waiting for the birth of his son.

"I really gotta dig deep and find inspiration to do this," he told himself. "I credit it to Nip, man," he said. "I think I had my antennas up and he helped direct it. Like he would with any other thing that we've done. A lot of the stuff was his genius that sparked it. And it's like, 'Okay, I know the execution part of it.' And 'How 'bout we do this?' or 'How about we do that?' So I think that series of billboards was no exception to that." He typed out the word "prolific," a word Hussle had tattooed on his face. A word Hussle used to describe himself in the first line of the song "Victory Lap." He positioned the word in capital letters from one side of the billboard to the other in the signature Marathon font, Franklin Gothic. "It seemed super fitting," he said. "And the photo, I put it as large as I could. I cut as carefully as I could around Nip with a pencil on Photoshop and positioned him, nestled him in between letters." In fifteen minutes the design was done. He sent it to the team and then his mother-in-law came to him and said, "Hey, your son's about to be born." They named the boy in Hussle's honour, Luis Ermias Peniche.

"I'm a man of faith and I believe that Nipsey's spirit lives with us," said the proud father. "And I see the many ways that he's pulling strings. Boy, man—this guy is doing' some phenomenal things for the people he loves and for his team. His impact will be forever remembered."

Peniche thinks of the billboards as a gift to the city. "People are healing and people are hurting," he said. "Nipsey represented more than a phenomenal artist but also a pillar of hope and, you know, like, an example that… 'I can do it too.' "

"After Nipsey got killed, it feels like the love is gone from over here," says Ralo. "I know I'm probably biased because that's my nigga, but it's definitely never gonna ever be the same over here. There's a void. It feels like the love left and like the lights went out."

Following Hussle's murder Ralo says he felt an anger come over him that he's never experienced before. "It was like the room would get still and quiet," he says. "I could've killed and eaten a sandwich right afterwards. I would have never mentioned it and it woulda never been... I had to pray to God that He would remove that heat from me. I was demonically angry," he adds with a mirthless laugh.

Fortunately Ralo was able to get out of town, spend some time in Atlanta, and get his head together. He did a lot of thinking about the choices both he and Ermias had made in their teen years. "It made me realise what was missing when I came off the porch," he says. "It was the fact that I didn't feel like that in my adolescence. Now when you feel like that at 13, I can't fathom it. Imagine your friend is murdered. You can't leave. You just have to walk right past that spot where your friend's blood was in the concrete. You gotta keep looking over your shoulders, you don't even know why. It puts so much hate in your heart you'll never get all that hate out. You'll never be the same. It's gonna physiologically change who you are."

Court proceedings for Eric Holder's murder trial have been delayed by the coronavirus. At a July 2020 pretrial hearing, he was brought into court shackled at the legs and wrist, and with chains around his waist. According to Alex Alonso, a gang expert and professor at California State University Long Beach, his yellow top and blue jumper pants indicated that he was in isolation and being held in a section known as High Power, where high-profile inmates are kept away from General Population. Holder was accompanied by defence attorney Lowynn Young, who has been representing him since Christopher Darden, famous for his role in prosecuting O.J. Simpson, resigned from this case due to death threats. There is a lot of hate out there for Eric Holder. Unconfirmed rumors circulate on the internet that several members of his family including his father have been killed or committed suicide, along with a plethora of conspiracy theories. At the hearing Holder's attorney told Judge Robert Perry that she had not been able to prepare a defence because she needed certain evidence in discovery but she had not been able to contact D.A. McKinney, who did not show up at court that day.

It's possible that Holder, who was apprehended outside a mental hospital, will never stand trial. He may plead insanity or strike a deal with prosecutors. Although the case has officially been solved, there are so many theories swirling on the internet, from pharmaceutical companies to an Illuminati sacrifice, it's already clear that Hussle's murder will join those of Malcolm X, JFK, Biggie, and Tupac in the file of unsolved mysteries.

"I've heard all of the conspiracy theories," says one LAPD detective who asked that his name be withheld so that he could speak freely. "You know, the baby momma, the Muslims... but I just say keep it simple. Just like Tupac—Tupac jumped on a guy, the guy went over there and shot him. But people want to make it seem like it was the FBI and all this kind of stuff." Nevertheless the detective believes that someone had to sanction the killing within the Rollin' 60s. "In gangs you do have to have the okay to pull the trigger," he says. "You can't pull a trigger on somebody like that and not risk some repercussions to you and your family. I do know that. Sometimes you gotta get the OK. 'Hey man I'm about to go do that.' And then handle your business or whatever."

Don't bother asking Ralo what happened to Nip. "I'm not willing to lose my life to answer that question," he says. Like Cuzzy and many of Hussle's closest friends, he doesn't buy the narrative that Hussle died in a random killing over a personal dispute with a member of the set.

"It just seemed like it's more than a fluke," says Cuzzy. "I'm not gonna say he was put up to it because I honestly don't know what the fuck happened. My mind thinks a million things. What I will say is this wasn't no fuckin' coincidence, man. That shit was heavily premeditated, I believe."

"It's just street shit," says Killa Twan. "It ain't none of this government's other extra bullshit they're trying to make. It's the everyday struggle we all go through out here in L.A. Just being a young Black man trying to do something positive and show people another way. Somebody's gonna hate you for whatever you do. And that's the sad part." Twan says he never heard of Shitty Cuz until the day of the killing. "It's nothing to be spoken about. It's just an inner circle thing and folks know what's what and how it's gonna get handled. It's that type of shit. None of this is old, 'Oh, the government, Dr. Sebi...' No. It's real street shit."

"Anybody that resembles a savior in the Black community is gunned the fuck down," Ralo tells me. "It is a narrative..." It's as if we know how the movie will end. And the idea that we can all accept that that is not what happened in order to maintain our normalcy is horrible. We have become unpleasant to me. We wouldn't have gone for this in the 1970s. "We wouldn't have gone for it in the 1990s."

One thing is certain: Nipsey Hussle did not die in vain. His impact is evident everywhere. Along with Tupac and Malcolm X, his visage has become a symbol of emancipation. Ralo asks what Nipsey Hussle's thoughts are on the 2020 national rebellion and aspirations for racial reconciliation. "I yearn to know what he would be doing right now—him and Kobe," he jokes. "Two of the most amazing people in our community. Two role models. Do you remember how it felt to be around people outside of the Black community at the time? Everyone's head was down. It felt like the wind was constantly knocked out of us. And then there's the Coronavirus. "We can't even breathe."

Ralo claims that Hussle's chains will wind up at the Smithsonian. When he received the news, he burst out laughing. "That's the second thing my homie did to impress me from the grave," Ralo tells me. The first was when he sent a cloud shaped like his face over Crenshaw and Slauson on the day of the memorial. "Everybody saw it," Ralo says. "Everyone was posting it. It was wonderful. There's no way I'd walk with a man and grow obsessed with him after he died. We weren't completely back on good terms. But it's so extraordinary that the entire narrative needs to be conveyed with that level of mystery," he laughs. "There is glittering dust, like fairy dust in the room right now, just cause I'm popping this shit."

He is astounded that Hussle "planned past his flesh" and kept his intentions intact. "That's a heavy duty business," Ralo says. "When you start talking about leaving a legacy, that word gets bandied about, but you have to really speak from the grave to do so. And the only way to accomplish so is if you were extremely focused while here. "He outlined this shit."

That example motivates people like Ralo to ensure that The Marathon continues. "We gotta carry the torch," he says. "It isn't even a marathon anymore. It is a relay. Nipsey Hussle definitely passed the baton to many individuals. He empowered a large number of people."

"Yes, they are scared of what we can do," Samantha Smith remarked on Instagram Live just before the 2020 election. "And they want us to always live below our potential. That is how they win. That is how they maintain power and control: by keeping us at the lowest control level. So, climb and don't be afraid, people. When you speak the truth, you will face a lot of blowback. Become a leader. Do not become a follower. If you have a strong conviction that something needs to be done, do not be discouraged by those around you. Simply do it. Please vote. "What do you have to lose?" Raising awareness of crucial topics and assisting voters is only one method to keep the Marathon moving. Sales of "FDT," her brother's YG protest anthem, increased by 1,200 percent during the election week. Streamed a million times on election day, the song inspired record turnout, particularly among Black voters, who eventually rejected Trump.

The last song released during Hussle's existence, "Racks in the Middle," featuring Roddy Ricch and Hit-Boy, received two Grammy Award nominations following his death. It has been his highest-charting song, debuting at number 44 on the Billboard Hot 100, boosted by a 2,776 percent increase in the artist's album sales following his murder—but some of the lyrics have changed. "I don't listen to that song," admits Jonny Shipes. "It breaks my heart."

In the song's second stanza, Hussle laments the death of his boyhood friend Fatts, and in the music video, Nipsey visits his friend's grave. "Damn, I wish my nigga Fatts was here," he rhymes. "How do you die at thirty-somethin' after bangin' all these years?"

Hussle freely acknowledged shedding tears in the studio while recording that stanza. Every bit as terrible as Hussle's statements about Fatts is the top of the song's second verse, when he declares, "Under no condition would you ever catch me slippin'." If only it were true, but people can't be hyper-vigilant all the time, especially in settings where they feel most comfortable.

"I wish I woulda been there," says the original Slauson Boy Hoodsta. Rob. Because things were different for me and my brother. Do you know? I was a member of the group, but I also observed him. G Bob was also watching him. I enjoyed everything, including the music. But I knew I was obliged to watch over my brother. So I was never so preoccupied with what was going on that I stopped paying attention to him. I wish I was there to jump in front of the rifle. However, everything happens for a purpose. That was my brother, and they knew that about me. You have to realise when you're part of something bigger."

"There's a certain air of 'Oh, but I'm here,'" Ralo exclaims. "And when you feel like that, you will let your guard down. And then you get there. So, whatever that implies. You become comfy, and then you are rocked to sleep.

"We were always conscious of playing defence and protecting ourselves," Hussle stated while discussing "Racks in the Middle" with the lyrics website Genius. "But then I had three full gun cases, so I don't play like that. I'm not out here jeopardising my daughter's safety like that. When I go to jail, everything will halt. Furthermore, hiring the gunman is less expensive than paying bail. Even if you win the lawsuit, the bail exceeds your pay, so we had to start thinking on those levels."

Nonetheless, on March 31, 2019, Nipsey Hussle arrived at his store—located in the shopping plaza that he, his older brother, and his business partner had recently purchased for $2.5 million—without any protection. As surveillance evidence clearly reveals, the shooter was able to fire on Hussle, run away, return to fire again, retreat again, then return a third time to fire the final shots before fleeing what should have been a suicidal act.

"That shit hurt me the most," recalls Rick Ross, who made legendary collaborations with Hussle and attempted to acquire him for Maybach Music Group. "Homie was out there wearing a white T-shirt and basketball shorts. This is similar to what happens at home. That is when you are at your most comfortable. Because I'm sure with one phone call, he could have had fifteen people, all black and armed with machine guns, standing there. On my mama, the last time I was with him, I was there, and as the sun began to set, he was so at ease, so at home, I thought maybe it was time for me to leave before I bought a certain vibe that wasn't there."

Ross understands the dangers of rising from hometown hero to nationally recognized rap artist. "When I move to certain places, it's not a secret," he jokes. "I'll have certain things in place. I want to be as comfortable as he was in my basketball shorts. And I've had the same attempts in my life. Not just once, not twice, but possibly more times than I can recall. But before you stop coming home, you say, 'Fuck it.' You have to do what you have to do, no matter how bad it seems. I still drive foreign cars through my neighbourhood because I believe it is my job. That's how I motivate young people because that's how I was inspired."

"For him to lose his life in the place he gave so much to, it's a life lesson for everyone," says Master P, the New Orleans music tycoon whose No Limit empire changed the game for independent rap labels, including Hussle's All Money In movement. "You still have to be able to understand the environment you are in because there are demons out there."

P was in the studio with Hussle two days before his death, recording the song "Street Millionaire" for the soundtrack to P's movie I Got the Hook-Up 2. "His mind was happy," P recalls. "He had just built a studio and he wanted everyone to see it. He was like, "Man, I did it!" I just acquired this building over here, I'm doing business, and I recently secured a shoe contract. He is making movements. He and his girlfriend had an excellent relationship. He has his children. He had everything going for him. I believe he was at his happiest moment. He didn't dislike anybody. If I called him, he'd remark, 'What you need, big dog?' No one could have predicted this. "The devil just arrived."

"Me and Nipsey got different mind frames," Meek Mill claimed in an interview with Charlamagne Tha God. "I think we were similar in certain aspects, but we had two completely distinct mental frameworks. "You ain't never see me back in the hood without a pistol around, close—and I'm talking about in a legal way," claimed the Philadelphia rapper, who wears a chain honouring Hussle and Lil Snupe, an artist signed to Meek's Dreamchasers imprint who was killed in 2013. "No young kings should be gunned down in the neighbourhood. He's a legend simply for that. You made it out, but you were gunned down by a lowlife. You are a legend; you have shown children that they can make it out, and someone from your past will draw you back and steal your life. I bet that Nipsey Hussle influenced hundreds of millions of slum children. They are well aware that pursuing their goals of remaining in the hood will endanger their lives. "Just that message alone."

Cuzzy Capone isn't ready to give up on the hood, but the loss of his companion has left him traumatised. "You've got to really handpick who you're fucking with, and make sure they're in control of their own life," he elaborates. "Make sure nothing is following them because that shit... You can see where it ends up. You see what happened in Bro's life. We've never been a city where producers and labels are eager to fuck with us or grab a nigga. It's wild-ass shit everywhere, but there's something about Los Angeles that's just not cool. Do you understand what I am saying? Niggas killed Biggie. Biggie died out here. Niggas killed Pac. Niggas murdered Nip. All of this stuff stems from L.A. niggas. The anger and evil in the street out here is so overwhelming, dude."

In the days following Hussle's death, tributes would take place in cities around the world. On Monday, April 1, Harlem artist Dave East, who worked with Hussle on songs such as "Clarity" starring Bino Rideaux, staged a candlelight vigil in New York City. Dave East, wearing a blue rag and holding a Mylar N balloon, wiped away tears as he paid respect to Hussle. "A sucka took out a fuckin' king," he was saying. "A true king for this era." I was a child when Pac and Big were together, so I couldn't relate. "I feel this shit." A group of mourners held candles and screamed, "Facts! Facts! Facts!" Dave East went on to declare, "I am no revolutionary nigga. I am not a preacher. I do not even do this. I am used to fucking shows. I don't do this shit. That is my brother. Do you smell me? "If no one else in New York City is going to do this, I will."

Nas, the iconic rapper who signed East to Mass Appeal Records and was admired by Hussle, was one of several celebrities to pay tribute to him on Instagram. "We are at a great loss today," he wrote. "It hurts. Straight to the point. It is perilous to be an MC. Being a basketball player is dangerous. It is dangerous to have money. It's dangerous to be a Black man. So much hate. We live as our brothers and sisters in third-world countries do. Right in America. Decisions concerning our own lives should be based on the possibility of death. It's so deeply rooted. It is not an easy repair. It's difficult to improve anything while children continue to live in poverty. But I'm not going to shut up. Nipsey has a genuine voice. He will not be silenced. He is still a stand-up General for the People who has never abandoned his people.

"All the memorial services around the world are just a testament to how many people he touched," Blacc Sam says. "It's a monument to his message, what he stood for, and how many people he inspired and affected. He was the actual people's champion, dude. The story is simply producing something out of nothing. And inspiring, never believing he was bigger, more exceptional, or better than everybody else. Simply sticking and demonstrating to others that if you believe and stick to your goals, you can always succeed. That was what everyone in every neighbourhood and region of the country admired, respected, and cherished about Nip. They're expressing their love, which is humbling."

"I feel like it's beautiful that so many people have been able to connect with such a special, chosen person," his younger sister, Samantha Smith, said. "It simply confirms the person he is." I always knew he was this type of person; I'm just glad the rest of the world knows too."

Iddris Sandu, All Money In's chief technological officer, takes up the torch and attempts to find a silver lining in this astonishing loss. "It's really interesting how everything is coming full circle now," he jokes. "When I use the term 'interesting' instead of 'tragic,' it's because I don't think something is tragic. It is truly a breakthrough. To say it's a tragedy implies that his message will not be continued. It's a breakthrough because so many individuals who were impacted by Nipsey Hussle, whether they met him or not, have come out to show their support. So for me, it's a breakthrough."

Could the end of such an extraordinary person's life be deemed a breakthrough? Perhaps, in a sense. Samantha, for one, cannot ignore the awful loss. "It also saddens me," she told me, "because at the end of the day not only do I feel like I lost such a significant person in my personal life, in our family, but I also feel like the whole world lost such a significant person too."

Gary Vaynerchuk, an entrepreneur and social media innovator, recalls how fast he and Nipsey Hussle became friends because of their shared interest in "creative destruction, the risky business of going against the grain." Despite coming from quite different backgrounds, Gary Vee noticed that he and Hussle both thought in fifty-year terms. "He wasn't as big as Pac and Biggie in the macro when this happened," Vaynerchuk told me. "But many people who had never heard of him were like, 'Wow! Why do the biggest names in the game continue to post so emotionally? Even if you only knew him briefly, he had an immediate impression on you."

"The meaning of Nip Hussle has taken on universal resonance and meaning now," said David Gross, the Los Angeles-born real estate investor and developer who supported the Asghedom brothers' acquisition of the plaza at Crenshaw and Slauson, giving them a foothold to lift themselves and their community. "People around the world get what he was."

His initiative "Our Opportunity" was intended to put the power of Opportunity Zones in the hands of people who cared about the well-being of the communities in which they invested. A year after Hussle's death, Gross had not abandoned their aims, but his perspective had grown with time. "I do want to get Tip, and I do want to get 2 Chainz, Meek, and [Allen Iverson]," he told Van Lathan at Vector90. "I want to bring together hometown heroes and buy up their cities for capital gains..." But it would not be true to my original vision that Nip and I had to continually work together to help the community."

Gross says he'd want to see the Opportunity Zone Act changed so that people of the 8,700 designated regions may obtain tax breaks for investing in their own communities, but until then, he's working with the tools that are now available. With the goal of "awakening people who have never invested before," Gross launched an Investor Challenge through Our Opportunity, awarding $100 awards to seed new accounts. Trae the Truth, a close friend of Hussle's, was among the first to reach out and offer his support. Others have now embraced the notion, which is spreading across the country. Meanwhile, Gross teaches fundamental economics and finance on Vector90's ground floor. Another effort, Own Our Own, invites neighbourhood residents to deposit $1,000 in a real estate investment fund.

"The same diligence I'll put into something that me and Nip would do, I'm putting into those deals," according to Gross. The ultimate goal is to "harness as much capital that is community-aligned, that is in the hands of people who care, who come from these neighbourhoods, so we can preserve the culture, so we don't displace." So we make certain that this investment, the money, is recycled into enterprises in our neighbourhood.

It's a former Wall Streeter's approach of remaining "ten toes down" and conducting finance in the Hussle style. If all goes as planned, Gross' work could become one of Hussle's most lasting legacies. "I'm not doing this for the community," he tells me. "I am doing this with the community.

Nipsey Hussle's mother is not mourning her son. She would prefer that people who loved him honour his memory and spirit. "I don't want you to be traumatised," she said to a schoolteacher who expressed her kids' sadness over Hussle's death. "I want you to know how glad I am, and that Ermias is with me right now. I can sense him. My son now understands the mysteries of life. Death should not be feared. Death is something you should prepare for. When you walk this earth, do nice things for others." Smith finds solace in the peaceful expression on her son's face when he was laid in his casket. "I looked at him and said, 'That's my angel baby.'" "Now he is a baby in the spirit world." Hussle's mother smiles as she comforts others in their pain. "Please don't stay down." Do not mourn. Nipsey Hussle has reached new heights, demonstrating his limitless potential. Ermias will not die. You hold him in your heart. Every moment you mention Ermias, he lives."

"As a father, I wish my son was still here with me," Dawit Asghedom remarked shortly after Ermias was laid to rest at Forest Lawn Cemetery in Hollywood Hills, which also has the graves of Michael Jackson, Walt Disney, John Singleton, and Rodney King. "But he has not died in vain. At barely 33 years old, he has already accomplished most of what he aimed for.Nobody imagined how much people loved and supported him. There are no words to explain. From the Marathon shop to the Staples Center, we marched through the streets. "It was incredible."

"We'll try to continue as much as we can," Blacc Sam remarked. Samantha, Nipsey Hussle's sister, confirms that his legacy will continue. "Definitely. Without a question. Without a question.

Councilmember Marqueece Harris-Dawson believes Nipsey's efforts will increase as his example encourages others. "I expect the Marathon store to prosper—and more importantly, the Marathon store concept," says the CEO. "I believe others will follow in his footsteps, as he has achieved financial success." People will come to South L.A., this neighbourhood, and the Crenshaw District to consume the culture that has been established here."

Nipsey was aware of the dangers of remaining so available to his area. He took those dangers as a self-made millionaire in the same way he had as a young Slauson Boy. "To be honest, that corner was known for robberies," he informed me the year before his death. "People would get robbed frequently on that corner. It's none of that now. My entire community understands that anyone who comes over here is there to promote the community's general well-being." Nipsey Hussle's reward for believing in his community was to die in front of the place he helped build. If his effort does not continue, his sacrifice will be in vain. And that would be much more tragic. Hussle has passed the torch—actually, multiple torches. For that reason alone, the Marathon must never end.

"Yeah, we're going to continue his legacy," says Iddris Sandu. "Everything he worked on. STEM project. Vector90. The destination is Crenshaw. The documentary. We will continue to do all of that.'Because he truly understood that it was not about him. It's actually for us."

Hussle reflected on his legacy in a Billboard interview from 2018. "I just want to impact the next 12-year-old Nip Hussle," he told me. "I want to make a difference in the lives of young men and women by passing on the wisdom I've gained along the way. I'll let them know and confirm their gut feelings. I want to be one of the voices or tales that say, "Nah, you're right." You are incredibly powerful. You have the greatest potential. I want to be one of those people that not only says it, but also demonstrates it."

"I'm a Black man first," declares the Black LAPD cop. "If you want to know what the police department thinks about Nipsey Hussle or how the policemen feel, I work with these people every day. They cannot laud a gang member. It doesn't matter that the Black community cares about what he's doing, giving back, and helping. But they can't let a gang member have that kind of structure over there representing him. And I conceal my feelings about it since I am aware of my location. I know where the hell I am. I'm not trying to come out here and hoist a Nipsey Hussle flag while working for the cops. They don't care if he gives back. To them, he is just a gang member and will always be that.

On his final visit to Big Boy's Neighborhood, Hussle reflected on his journey and summed up the Marathon's resilient spirit. "We got turned down," he remarked. "We failed. Had setbacks. Had to start again several times. You know, but we kept at it. That is always the deciding factor in any situation. The brand's name is, unsurprisingly, Marathon. It just stands for endurance. It stands for "stay down.""

Big Boy questioned if he had ever lost faith. "Did you ever feel like, 'Man, this ain't gonna work'?"

"That's why I call my thing the Marathon," Hustle explained. "I'm not going to lie and act like I've got it all together. Nah. I just didn't quit. That's the only distinguishing feature. I experienced every emotion. And I believe that what will distinguish those who attempt to achieve something is their refusal to give up. You're going to take the posture of, 'I'm going to die because of what I'm getting at right now.'"

In the same spirit, Blacc Sam has pledged to complete the Nipsey Hussle Tower, a mixed-use residential complex that will include affordable housing, a renovated flagship store for The Marathon Clothing, and a Nipsey Hussle museum.

"Nipsey was a true inspiration for the have-nots," Sam stated in response to the Los Angeles city attorney's efforts to close The Marathon Clothing business. "He was the people's champion." He rose from nothing to triumph. He excelled in difficult situations. He had complete respect from the streets. Because he [led] by example, honour and responsibility were always his moral compass....

"Regardless of anyone's efforts to prevent this from happening, Nipsey's desire will be realised and carried down to his progeny. The Nipsey Hussle Tower will inspire and demonstrate to people that even if you start from nothing, you can achieve greatness. History will tell the story of Nipsey Hussle. The Nipsey Hussle tower will be erected, and his legacy will live on in stone and in people's hearts forever."

It is early afternoon on Slauson Avenue. Tourists are rushing to take photographs with the larger-than-life Nipsey Hussle paintings in the lane by the Fatburger that connects Slauson Avenue and Fifty-Eighth Place. This is the same alley that the appropriately called Shitty Cuz went down on March 31, 2019, with two pistols and wearing a hood. The question of whether Eric Holder was recruited by cops, put up to it by the hood, or acted alone out of envious wrath will most likely be discussed indefinitely. Ultimately, the loss remains the same. The murder of Neighborhood Nip was a crime against humanity.

"I'm praying for him, too," Hussle's grandma says. "I pray he is not killed in captivity. He has enough time to seek God's forgiveness. I am a Catholic. I believe in prayers, and I am praying for him. He was in a youthful, stupid circumstance, and I hope he regrets what he did."

Few people feel the loss as strongly as Slauson Bruce. He was down and out when Hussle first hired him to maintain the parking lot. Today, Bruce is waiting for a business meeting, sitting on a small red concrete wall just outside the locked chain-link fence that now surrounds the entire parking lot at 3420 West Slauson Ave, which was once a thriving commercial hub, the Marathon Clothing smart store. Next to Bruce is a shopping cart full with miscellaneous items. Bruce, dressed in an Adidas tracksuit and a worn-out black fedora, takes a few minutes to speak.

"I did a lot," Bruce explains. "I constructed this building, guy. I'm telling you. I used to steam clean this lot. It's all kinds of garbage. Wash the windows. It's only me, really. Nipsey would not be here. He'd be in the studio. He'd leave Sam, his brother, Fatts, and the others in charge." Bruce coughs hard and continues. "He replied he would not have time for it. He had to create tunes."58

When Bruce met Nipsey, he was riding his bike and collecting cans. "Fifteen long years ago," he recalls, recalling the life-changing event vividly. "He backed his car out, and when he backed out he thought I was in the way."

Nipsey opened the door.

"Are you all right?" he inquired.

"I replied, 'Yes.'" "I need a job."

"You keep this lot clean, you got one," Nipsey warned him. That was in 2004, and Nipsey Hussle was somewhat unknown outside of the Crenshaw District. Slauson Bruce claims he's been here ever since.

"You damn right," he responds when asked if he could tell Hussle was special.

Hussle recognized something in Bruce, and the two created a bond.

"So we went on and on and talked," Bruce explains. "And he said, 'Wait a minute, I'ma put you in a movie!'" True to his word, Nipsey Hussle cast Slauson Bruce to star in "The Midas Touch," a YouTube video released on February 1, 2018, as part of the Victory Lap album rollout. In the ten-minute video, Bruce abandons the shopping cart and enters Nipsey Hussle's Maybach. Bruce receives a new haircut at the Shave Parlor on Slauson and Seventh Avenue, and a charcoal-grey suit from Tom Ford in Beverly Hills. He goes to the jewellery store for a gold ring, watch, bracelet, and chain, then has a manicure and massage. Bruce indulges in a lobster dinner with part of the All Money In staff before heading to a high-end strip club.

Everything has altered since March 31. "Since then, it's not been too good," says Bruce. "I can't sleep at night." His dog, Pet Bull, glances at Bruce, who looks back.

"I break out crying every night," he says. "But I stated there's nothing I could do about it. What he told me before he died: he was parking and leaving and remarked, 'The Marathon continues.' I said I'll make sure of that.Because he has done so much for us.

Bruce had cleaned up the property on the day Nipsey Hussle was slain. "I had just left," he continued, his voice softer than usual. "I don't hang around here. I used to hang around, but as time passed, I stopped doing so. I'd arrive at six o'clock to tidy up the lot. Then I worked at Woody's. Then, at night, I'd go clean up elsewhere. "Three jobs per day—man!"

All of those positions are now gone. Bruce's girlfriend died two years ago in her sleep. "I been goin' through all type of shit," he's saying. Since then, he has lost some of his marathon momentum. "I ain't doing' nothing," he adds, casting his gaze up Slauson Ave toward Crenshaw. "I can't find nothing." But he hopes Blacc Sam will repair the place. "That's why it's gated," Bruce explains. "They're building it up, making apartments."

Just then, a lady from across the street arrives on foot. She claims she saw Nipsey's godbrother Adam a few blocks away.

"Where?"

"At the place."

"Talk to him?"

"Not this time." She hands Bruce some money and walks back the way she came. The hustling never stops.

"That was my sister just now," Bruce says. "She delivered some orders from Chicago. A friend of hers had ordered some shirts. They're not even available for purchase online. They backed up. "You can't get any."

If Bruce could say anything to Nipsey right now, it would be: "Hey, man, the Marathon continues. "Believe it or not."

Yes, it does continue. Even with the padlocked gate, barbed wire, and solid green fabric concealing anything from view. The fence was erected on August 1, 2019, to deter unwelcome guests from loitering on the lot where the Marathon Clothing business still remains. The cops are constantly on the lookout for someone to make a mistake and bring Nipsey Hussle's team down. Nipsey Hussle's followers remain undeterred, turning out on a daily basis. In the months since his death, fans from all over the world have been to this location, taking selfies, praying, and scrawling innumerable messages in his honour—RIP Nip, TMC 4Ever, Hussle The Great!—on every available square inch of wall and window space.

This shopping complex at 3420 West Slauson Ave is now holy ground, just as it was for Nipsey, Sam, Adam, and Fatts in their lives. A prophet's blood was spilled here, and no gate is tall enough to keep out all the love. Nipsey Hussle is the people's champion, and everyone knows it, but the Los Angeles City Attorney's Office does not see it that way.

"We bought the lot, man," Sam said proudly during his brother's memorial service on April 11 at the Staples Center. "I'm not sure how we did it." And that was a big deal for bro, dude, because he used to sell CDs from his trunk. He used to be in that parking lot, and they'd try to kick him out. And you guys know what we went through with the cops in that lot."60

Bruce witnessed the conflict several times over his years of employment with the family firm. "When the cops arrived and tore the place down, Sam informed me—what did he say? Oh, 'The great retribution.' He created this sucker in just two days. 'They will not stop me!' That is what he said. And everything is legal. They weren't selling any dope. They're looking for guns and stuff. They didn't carry that crap. "They were going legit."

Bruce has no patience for conspiracy theories. If you ask him who killed Nipsey Hussle, he will tell you straight up: "What you call a hater," he says. "You're a jealous motherfucker. That's what I believe.

But what about the fact that he was allegedly someone Hussle knew?

"Your best friend could be a jealous motherfucker."

Blacc Sam has continued to fight in court to preserve his brother's legacy and protect his family's interests. Crips LLC filed trademark applications for Hussle's tagline "The Marathon Continues" on May 16, less than two months after his death, including one for the ability to use it on clothes. Sam submitted a similar trademark application on May 28. When Sam spoke out publicly, a spokeswoman for Crips LLC issued an apology in July 2019. "There will absolutely be no trademark legal battle between their organisation and Blacc Sam, brother of the late Nipsey Hussle," the statement stated, adding that the organisation recognized the application could be "offensive" and has contacted the family. However, actions speak louder than words.

Because Crips LLC would not drop its application, Nipsey Hussle's estate filed a lawsuit in October 2020, requesting monetary damages and a court order requiring the firm to remove all unlawful Marathon items.

Hussle spoke with Complex in 2013, after making one hundred racks in one night at the inaugural Crenshaw pop-up shop, on why Nipsey Hussle fans felt so strongly. "Because I'm real, my nigga," he said. "My tale is authentic. There are no rap niggas in the game like me. Especially among my generation. No nigga has ever stood up to what I have. I went through that. I thought as I thought. Did not give up. Stayed down and in the shit. Built for his neighbourhood. Stayed local and motivated his community. Came from a dangerous environment, such as the Rollin' 60s. I confronted killers head on. There is no nigga in the game like me. So that's what they're drawn to, as well as the fact that my music allows me to express myself."

Down the street from Slauson Bruce, Reverend Abdullah, a clean-cut young brother in a neat coat and tie, sells copies of The Final Call, the Nation of Islam's newspaper. The paper's April 9, 2019, issue included a cover article titled "The Life, Loss, and Legacy of Nipsey Hussle." During the week of Hussle's burial, the NOI distributed 100,000 copies of the issue throughout Los Angeles. When Minister Louis Farrakhan spoke during Hussle's nationally televised tribute at the Staples Center, he claimed Nipsey "is to hip-hop and rap what Bob Marley was to reggae; he is the prophetic voice of all in that community."

"He never said no to the paper—him or his brother," Reverend Abdullah explains. "Never say no."

If there is anything positive to come out of the March 31, 2019, tragedy, Reverend Abdullah believes it is the spotlight it has cast on the Crenshaw District and the work Hussle was doing here. "It's certainly an unfortunate circumstance. However, people are becoming more conscious of what is going on in their communities. The brother's death isn't necessarily a good thing. But at the very least, many people are aware of what he was doing, his message, and the issues."

Reverend Abdullah has been selling the paper in the commercial complex on Slauson and Crenshaw since before Hussle died. "One hundred percent," he says. "A familiar face to him. We had several chats. We saw each other in different places. That's why I wanted to conduct an interview, since I adored him. "Heck yeah."

He can recall the first time he met Hussle. "It was right over there," he replies, pointing at the parking lot. "It was astonishing how approachable he was, and how he was actually doing what he said on the streets. He wasn't one of those rappers that made things up, like a lifestyle. When I met him, he had a shoebox filled with money. He stopped counting the shoebox to buy paper, then resumed again. I'm not sure what the deal was, but that's the type of person he is. So that's exactly what I want the world to know.

What will people learn from what happened to him? "I think people should keep giving back," adds Reverend Abdullah. "I believe people should just learn. I am unable to tell you my lesson. I learned thousands of lessons from it. It's like some books. I cannot tell you what it means; you must read it. But you should definitely invest in the community. Keep doing it. Pick up from where he left off. He gave T.I. the book "Message to the Blackman in America." Pick up where he left off.

If he could tell Hussle one thing, it would be, "I love you. I adore you, brother. That is it. 100 percent. "Thanks, Nipsey Hussle."

Made in United States
Troutdale, OR
07/25/2024

21524604R00076